DEATH TO BOURGEOIS SOCIETY

The Propagandists of the Deed

Revolutionary Pocketbooks

DEATH TO BOURGEOIS SOCIETY

The Propagandists of the Deed

**Edited and translated by
Mitchell Abidor**

Death to Bourgeois Society: The Propagandists of the Deed
Edited and translated by Mitchell Abidor
This edition copyright © 2015 PM Press
All rights reserved. No part of this book may be transmitted by any
means without permission in writing from the publisher.

ISBN: 978-1-62963-112-7

Library of Congress Control Number: 2015930907

Cover by John Yates/Stealworks
Layout by Jonathan Rowland based on work by briandesign

10 9 8 7 6 5 4 3 2 1

PM Press
PO Box 23912
Oakland, CA 94623
www.pmpress.org

Printed in the USA by the Employee Owners of Thomson-Shore in
Dexter, Michigan. www.thomsonshore.com

■ CONTENTS

■ INTRODUCTION

No brief period has so marked a political movement as the years 1892–94 did for French anarchism. Those years, with their wave of bombings by anarchist militants, fixed the image of anarchists as wild-eyed bomb throwers, an image the press and the government did all in its power to impress on the public.

Though there is no question that the bombings were often aimed at targets of no political significance, such as cafés and restaurants, the acts of the bombers, of Ravachol, Auguste Vaillant, Émile Henry, and the assassin Santo Caserio, were in no way unmotivated acts of unthinking, goalless terror. As the documents in this anthology show, they and their comrades were motivated by the noblest of ideals and their deeds were intended as acts of propaganda aimed at inspiring mass activity.

The three years of anarchist terror had actually been germinating for some time. The first act of propaganda of the deed was committed in Italy in 1872. In 1881, the International Anarchist Congress held in London, attended by Louise Michel as a representative from France, gave the tactic its approval.

Only the occasional anarchist bomb exploded over the next few years, but in 1892 the pattern truly took hold. The first of the propagandists of the deed was Ravachol. Born in

1859 as François Koenigstein to a Dutch father and a French mother (his name leading anti-Semites to assume he was a Jew), he was forced to work from a young age as a hired hand and an apprentice dyer after his father abandoned the family. At age eighteen, Ravachol read Eugene Sue's *The Wandering Jew* and abandoned religion. Soon thereafter, he began frequenting anarchist circles, which (as was frequently the case) cost him his job when his boss discovered his activities. Ravachol then took up crime as a livelihood, working up from petty larceny to major theft. In the late 1880s, he also worked as a songwriter and musician, one of his songs (included below) bearing the title "Liberté, Egalité, Fraternité."

Though he paid for his career as a criminal with his life, Ravachol the anarchist far overshadowed Ravachol the criminal. He placed his first bomb on March 11, 1892, at the home of the judge presiding over a trial of anarchists, which caused damage to the building but no injuries. In a related bombing on March 27, he planted a device at the home on the Rue de Clichy of the prosecuting attorney who had called for death for the same group of anarchists. No one was killed or wounded, but the property damage was more serious this time.

Between these two attacks, a bomb was detonated at the Lobau Barracks on March 15. This time, the police considered Ravachol a suspect, sending his description to the press. On the day of the bombing on the Rue de Clichy, Ravachol had gone to eat at the Restaurant Véry, talking to the waiter about anarchism and the bombing, news of which had not yet been disseminated. When he returned to the restaurant two days later, the waiter recognized the scar on his hand that was mentioned in the police description and contacted the local commissariat. It took ten officers to control him and bring him in.

Justice was swift. On April 26, barely four weeks after his arrest, the trial began in a climate of fear in a heavily guarded courtroom. On the previous day, a bomb had exploded in the restaurant where Ravachol was captured; two people were killed, including the owner of the establishment. Ravachol was tried along with four other anarchists, but he assumed sole responsibility for all the acts committed. He explained that all of the bombings were in response to government brutality and repression. Contrary to all expectations, only Ravachol and one of the other defendants were found guilty. Thanks to Ravachol's stand at the trial, the other three were acquitted.

Simon, the other defendant found guilty, was later killed in a revolt in the penal colony to which he was sent. Ravachol the anarchist escaped with his life. But on June 21, Ravachol the criminal stood trial for the murder of an aged rentier and his housekeeper; for robbing the grave of the Comtesse de la Rochetaillée; for the murder of Jacques Brunel, called the "Hermit of Chambles"; and for the murder of two shopkeepers. With the exception of the first of these crimes, which dated from 1886, the other three had all taken place between May and July 1891.

Ravachol accepted responsibility for the grave-robbing and the murder of the hermit, explaining that he hadn't expected to find the hermit at home and in his surprise had had no choice but to kill, but denied having committed any other murders. His explanation for his thefts was one that would later become familiar in the heyday of illegalism: he stole to obtain what he needed to survive and what honest labor couldn't obtain for him, as well as in order to assist the anarchist cause.

When his death sentence was announced, Ravachol greeted it with the cry of "Vive l'Anarchie!" When he walked to the guillotine on July 11, he sang a profane song calling for the death of priests and bourgeois ("If you want to live a happy life/hang your boss/and cut the priests in two"). His final cry of "Vive la Ré . . ." was cut off by the blade before he completed the word "révolution."

As the selections in this anthology show, Ravachol's courage in the face of his judges impressed anarchist and anarchist-leaning writers alike, and they wrote in praise of him, likening him to Jesus and calling him a saint. Appeals for vengeance were issued, echoing his words at his trial: "I've made the sacrifice of my person. If I'm still fighting it's for the anarchist idea. It's of no importance to me if I'm condemned; I know I'll be avenged."

Despite the expectation of revenge, a period of calm followed Ravachol's execution. But on December 9, 1893, the heart of the government was struck when a bomb was tossed from the spectators' gallery onto the floor of the Chamber of Deputies. No one was killed, and the session soon picked up where it had left off. Twenty anarchists were rounded up as suspects, but the next morning August Vaillant, who had been wounded in the explosion and was being treated at the Hôtel-Dieu Hospital, admitted his guilt and was questioned at his bedside. His interrogation is included in this anthology.

Up to this point, Vaillant had led a difficult existence. Born in poverty in the Ardennes in 1861, he moved to Paris on his own at the age of twelve. He was arrested for begging and theft, and by the age of fifteen was an apprentice pastry

4

chef, soon leaving that to work as a cobbler, a thermometer maker, and a laborer. He gravitated toward anarchism, but the difficulty of his existence led him to expatriate with his wife to Argentina in 1890. According to Vaillant's own account, he worked as a French tutor there; other accounts have him working as a farmer. In either case, he returned to Paris in 1893, where he lived in abject poverty with a mistress and Sidonie, his daughter from his marriage (his wife remained in Argentina). In his anger and frustration, he resolved to bomb . . . something. Provided with funds by an illegalist comrade and the wife of the anarchist Paul Reclus (who would soon be a defendant in the Trial of the Thirty that grew out of the government reaction to Vaillant's bombing attack), Vaillant rented a room where he built the bomb he threw in the Chamber of Deputies.

After the attack, the government went into a frenzy and passed the *lois scélérates*, "villainous laws," which banned anarchist propaganda, and did all it could to make Vaillant's defense at his trial impossible. The trial, which lasted only one day, took place on January 10, 1894.

Though no one was killed and a priest wounded in the attack appealed for clemency, Vaillant was sentenced to death. Like Ravachol, he shouted "Vive l'Anarchie!" when the sentence was handed down.

Despite all attempts to convince President Sadi Carnot (grandson of the French Revolution's National Convention member Lazare Carnot, who had voted to execute Louis XVI), including a letter from Vaillant's daughter Sidonie to Carnot's wife, Vaillant was executed on February 5, 1894. On his way to the guillotine he shouted "Vive l'Anarchie! My death will be avenged!" His final words were "Death to bourgeois society and long live anarchy!" His last wish was that Sidonie be raised by Sébastien Faure, one of the leading figures of French anarchism. This was done, and when she later married, one of the conditions of the marriage was that she change her name and have nothing to do with anarchism or anarchists ever again. This, too, was done.

Carnot, though, had signed his own death sentence when he refused to pardon Vaillant, and was now a dead man walking. Exactly a week after Vaillant's execution, Émile Henry tossed at bomb in the Café Terminus at the Gare Saint-Lazare. Captured at the scene of the attack, he spent his first three days in custody providing the police with false information about his name and address, thus giving comrades a chance to dispose of the material in his apartment that he had planned to use to make at least a dozen more bombs. When he finally gave his name, he also admitted to being responsible for a bomb that had exploded after being transported to the commissariat on the Rue des Bons-Enfants on November 8, 1892, a bomb that killed five people.

This device had originally been placed on the landing against the door of the offices of the Société des Mines de Carmaux on the Avenue de l'Opéra. When the device was noticed, it was carried to the police station where the explosion occurred. Not only did Henry take credit for the attacks, but he aided the prosecution: when questions were raised as to how it was possible for him to have crisscrossed Paris on that day in the limited amount of time all of it took, he himself provided proof of his ability to traverse the city as he did, and thus of his guilt. His fate was a foregone conclusion: On May 21, 1894, he went to the guillotine, shouting "Courage, comrades! Vive l'Anarchie!"

Henry's road to the guillotine differed markedly from those of Vaillant and Ravachol and does much to enlighten us concerning the reasons behind this outbreak of terror at that particular moment. His father, Fortuné, was a Communard sentenced to death in absentia, and Émile was born during the family's exile in Spain in 1872. Unlike Ravachol and Vaillant, Henry was a prize-winning student, but he abandoned (or, according to some accounts, failed in) the scholarly life. While engaging in anarchist propaganda (he wrote for several anarchist papers), he worked at various commercial trades. Not only did Henry come from a political background, but he had the opportunity to express his opinion of propaganda of the deed as a writer, roundly condemning it as a tactic. He harshly criticized Ravachol in particular, saying that acts such as Ravachol's bombings "do us great harm." Significantly, however, he added that "a real anarchist kills his enemy; he doesn't dynamite houses where there are women, children, and domestics," thus articulating an opportunity for violent activity when properly carried out. This was written on March 18, 1892. By August, Henry had changed his point of view, arguing that bombings were a way "to awaken the masses, shake them up with the lash of a whip, and show them the vulnerability of the bourgeoisie."

For Henry—as for Ravachol, as for Vaillant—violent acts did not simply respond to his personal needs. Unlike the later anarchist individualists who showed no concern for the masses or their problems and instead demonstrated a sneering contempt for the plebe, Henry and his fellows saw their acts as part of (and as detonators of) the mass struggle they viewed as necessary for the success of the revolution. Though they acted alone (or at most with a handful of co-conspirators), much like the Russian Populists who served as an inspiration, they were a kind of vanguard party of one, hoping to show the masses the way and to shake them out of their torpor. The later individualists (such as Victor Serge, whose youthful article in commemoration of Henry is included in this anthology) saw the masses as hopeless and revolution as a sham, and their involvement in violence was almost solely in the form of illegalism. The rampage of the Bonnot Gang in 1910–11, with pointless deaths among both the public and the anarchists, demonstrated that this path was a dead end. Whatever the propagandists of the deed and the individualists might seem to have in common, such as their shared belief in the efficacy of action by the lone fighter, they were in reality at antipodes from each other. Both acted out of frustration. But while the terrorists' frustration was the result of a quiescence they hoped was temporary, the individualists viewed this quiescence as the permanent state of the masses. The propagandists of the deed's violent acts were revolutionary, both an end and a means toward that end; for the individualists, their positive effect on the One committing them was enough.

The bombing wave was about to reach its end, but not before an attack with a certain irony. On April 4, 1894, a bomb placed at the Restaurant Foyot killed no one, but cost the writer Laurent Tailhade an eye. Tailhade had defended Ravachol, saying, "What difference do the victims make as long as the act is beautiful?" Even more ironically, the bomb was likely planted by Tailhade's friend, the writer Félix Fénéon, one of the thirty anarchists soon to be tried after the passing of the *lois scélérates.*

On June 24, the anarchists wreaked the ultimate revenge. Twenty-one-year-old Santo Caserio, an Italian immigrant who had been active in anarchist circles since the age of eighteen, had decided to carry out a "great exploit." He purchased a dagger (legend has it that the name "Vaillant" was inscribed on it) and travelled from his hometown of Cette to Lyon, where he had read the president of the Republic was paying a visit. With no great difficulty (the act itself is described in his own words in this anthology), he was able to approach the president and, avenging Vaillant, sunk his dagger into the president's chest. The ease with which Caserio was able to carry out his act led people to believe that a many-tentacled anarchist network had arranged it all, and that the prefect of Lyon had received warning that such an attack was planned. But as we have learned in our own time, a lone wolf is hard to foil.

As he killed the president, Caserio shouted, "Vive la Révolution! Vive l'Anarchie!" At his execution on August 15, 1894, his last words were "Vive l'Anarchie!"

* * *

Overall, there were eleven bombings throughout this era that resulted in eleven deaths, and the assassination of the president. The vengeance of the government was far harsher than that of the anarchists: as mentioned above, within two days of Vaillant's act, the so-called *lois scélérates* were passed, banning almost all anarchist activity and propaganda, and closing down the entire anarchist press. On August 6, 1894, the Trial of the Thirty began, calling out the leading figures of French anarchism such as Sébastien Faure, Jean Grave, and Félix Fénéon. Some, such as Émile

Pouget, had fled to avoid the trial. Along with these theoreticians and militants, a large group of illegalists was among the defendants. The attempt to tar the entire anarchist movement with the illegalist brush failed, and only three of the defendants, all illegalists, were found guilty.

After this, anarchist terrorism waned in importance. It had flared up suddenly as a result of the lack of large-scale militancy and in response to the scandal-ridden Third Republic. This was the era of the Panama Scandal, when the collapse of the French attempt to build the canal resulted in the loss of millions of francs fraudulently squandered, which itself was nothing but a symptom of the general degradation of the Republic, soon to be all the more glaring in the anti-Semitism of the Dreyfus Affair. Bourgeois society daily demonstrated the rot at its core and it deserved to be destroyed. The propagandists of the deed were trying to do just that, one bomb at a time. The courage with which Ravachol, Henry, Vaillant, and Caserio proclaimed their guilt made them heroic figures against this backdrop of tawdriness, dishonesty, and moral degradation. The bombings ended when they did, not only because the tactic seemed futile but because by 1894 mass revolutionary movements, particularly revolutionary syndicalism, were growing in strength. This wave dominated anarchism in the years to come. The terrorists' job was done and they could withdraw from the scene.

What follows in this volume is a portrait of that era, of that moment in anarchist history, in the words of the actors. Actors proud of their acts and anxious to explain and justify them.

Further Reading:

The library of books in English on the propagandists of the deed is a thin one. Barbara Tuchman, in her *The Proud Tower*, wrote of the bombings in her usual entertaining fashion, but not with any great depth. Fortunately, in 2009 John Merriman published his excellent and thorough *The Dynamite Club*, and in 2010 Alex Butterworth published his study, *The World That Never Was*, both of which treat the subject with as much depth, insight, and accuracy as any of the French sources. They are absolutely essential and a great read.

Joseph Conrad's *The Secret Agent* has as its background one of the strangest acts of the period, the failed attempt by the French anarchist Martial Bourdin to blow up the Greenwich Observatory, the home of Greenwich Mean Time. No one could ever confuse Conrad with an anarchist, but this is a fascinating portrait of the time and the mentality. The historical background of the novel, in particular the life of Bourdin, is masterfully laid out by Mary Burgoyne in her essay "Conrad Among the Anarchists" in the Spring 2007 issue of *The Conradian*. Burgoyne's essay is a remarkable piece of historical detective work.

Propagandists of the deed worked in other countries and at other times. Paul Avrich in his *Sacco and Vanzetti: The Anarchist Background* recounted the insufficiently known story of the Italian anarchist bombers with whom the two martyrs worked. And there were also important groups of this kind in Argentina in the twentieth century, operating as late as the 1920s, and their story is told by the historian of Argentine anarchism Osvaldo Bayer in two short books that have been translated into English,

Anarchism and Violence: Severino Di Giovanni in Argentina and his book on Simon Radowitzky, *Simon Radowitzky and the People's Justice.*

Mitchell Abdor

■ RAVACHOL

A Narrative

Editor's note: Three autobiographical texts by Ravachol date from his time in prison just prior to his execution on July 11, 1892. The first is an account of his most notorious crime, his attempt at grave-robbing; the second is a longer fragment about his youth, political development, and criminal life; and the last is an account dictated to the police, "My Principles." This first text, supposedly written in his own hand, complete with grammatical and spelling mistakes, appeared in a Parisian paper two days after Ravachol's death.

"Among the papers left by Ravachol is found the story of the violation of the grave of Mme la baronne de Rochetaillée. Someone who momentarily had it in his possession having sent it to us, we reproduce it in its entirety, respecting the spelling and grammar. The story is written with a cold and tranquil cynicism, which will inspire in readers the same horror we ourselves felt."
—*Le Gaulois*, July 13, 1892

. . . being without work I set myself to making false money, a means not very lucratif and but dangerous, so I soon abbandonned it. I learnd that there was a baroness named de Rochetaillée who had bin buried not to long before. I thought she must have some jewels on her, so I resolved to break into the toomb.

One day I got myself a hooded lamp and a jimmy and I set out.

I left home at nine at night. Along the way I went into a bakery with the intenshun of paying the owner with a two frank piece in exchange for a loaf of bred, but he reconized that it was false. I pretended not to no this and continued along my way. Further along I went into a café and asked for a drink to take with me and I managed to give the owner a two frank piece. Further along I went again to a baker, I asked for a small loaf, I gave him a two frank piece and went on my way.

I got to the cematary at eleven. Before going in I ate my bred and drank some wine, and climb the wall and head for the grave that I attentively inspect.

So using my jimmy I lifted the toombstone and I entered the toomb; seeing the name I was looking for on a marble stone I set myself to unsealing it with the jimmy. So that the stone shouldn't fall on me I went into an empty compartment beside it. In falling the stone made a great noise and it broke into many pieces.

I quickly went back up to see if anyone was passing by. Not seeing anything suspishus, I went back down. I broke the three or four circles that closed the coffin. It wasn't easy to do this.

Afterward I tried to fit my jimmy into a joint in the coffin and was able to do so. I bust open the planks by pressing on them, but there was a layer of led wrapped around the corpse. I banged on it with the point of the jimmy and managed to make an opening big enough to take out the arm to see her left hand. I had to take out several small pakages which I didn't know what they contained. Once her left arm was out I pulled it too me and looked attentively at the fingers which was covered with mold. I didn't find what I was looking for. I looked at the throat and didn't see nothing there neither, and since my lamp didn't light anymore since it had no more oil, in order to finish my operation I set on fire a wreath of flowers I'd found in a chapel over the fault. It spred a thick smoke as it berned which caused me to go rush back up if I didn't want to asfixiate.

When I opened the coffin I had only one fear and that was that a large escaping of asfixiating gas would take place, but because I was in a hurry do to a certain need I didn't hesitate because its preferable to die risking yourself than succumming to hunger.

Once I climbed up I put the toombstone back in place and I started back home but on leaving I saw about a hundred meters away two men coming across the fields who seemed to want to cut me off in order to stop me.

I put my hand on my revolver and slowed down a little. They passed in front of me not saying anything. Later, on the Rue da la Monta, I meet a man at about a hundred meters who asked the way to the Chateau Creux. I didn't clearly understand him and he came up to me and repeated the question. I told him to follow me, that I passed write by it. He said to me that I was wearing a fake beard on my face which made me smile since I thought I had nothing to fear from this man who was all alone.

This happened on the Rue de la Monta. Coming up on the station I showed him the way and continued on mine. I went back home.

Ravachol's Forbidden Speech

Editor's note: On trial for murder after a series of bombings, Ravachol attempted to give the following speech, not to deny his guilt but to accept and explain it. According to contemporary accounts, he was cut off after a few words and the speech was never delivered. He was guillotined shortly afterward.

If I speak, it's not to defend myself for the acts of which I'm accused, for it is society alone that is responsible, since by its organization it sets man in a continual struggle of one against the other. In fact, don't we see today, in all classes and all positions, people who desire, I won't say the death, because that doesn't sound good, but the ill fortune of their fellows if they can gain advantages from this? For example, doesn't a boss hope to see a competitor die? And don't all businessmen reciprocally hope to be the only one to enjoy the advantages that their occupations bring? In order to obtain employment, doesn't the unemployed worker hope that for some reason or another someone who *does* have a job will be thrown out of his workplace. Well then, in a society where such things occur, there's no reason to be surprised about the kind of acts for which I'm blamed, which are nothing but the logical consequence of the struggle for existence that men carry on who are obliged to use every means available in order to live. And since it's every man for himself, isn't he who is in need reduced to thinking: "Well, since that's the way things are, when I'm hungry I have no reason to hesitate about using the means at my disposal, even at the risk of causing victims! Bosses, when they fire workers, do they worry whether or not they're going to die of hunger? Do those who have a surplus worry if there are those who lack the basic necessities?"

There are some who give assistance, but they are powerless to relieve all those in need who will either die prematurely because of privations of various kinds, or voluntarily by suicides of all kinds, in order to put an end to a miserable existence and to not have to put up with the rigors of hunger, with countless shames and humiliations, and who are without hope of ever seeing them end. Thus there are the Hayem and Souhain families, who killed their children so as not to see them suffer any longer, and all the women who, in fear of not being able to feed a child, don't hesitate to destroy in their wombs the fruit of their love.

And all these things happen in the midst of an abundance of all sorts of products. We could understand if these things happened in a country where products are rare, where there is famine. But in France, where abundance reigns, where butcher shops are loaded with meat, bakeries with bread, where clothing and shoes are piled up in stores, where there are unoccupied lodgings! How can anyone accept that everything is for the best in a society when the contrary can be seen so clearly? There are many people who will feel sorry for the victims, but who'll tell you they can't do anything about it. Let everyone scrape by as he can! What can he who lacks the necessities when he's working do when he loses his job? He has only to let himself die of hunger. Then people will throw a few pious words on his corpse. This is what I wanted to leave to others. I preferred to make of myself a trafficker in contraband, a counterfeiter, a murderer, and an assassin. I could have begged, but it's degrading and cowardly and even punished by your laws, which make poverty a crime. If all those in need, instead of waiting *took*, wherever and by whatever means, the self-satisfied would perhaps understand a bit more quickly that it's dangerous to want to consecrate the existing social state, where worry is permanent and life threatened at every moment.

We can immediately see that the anarchists are right when they say that in order to have moral and physical peace the causes that give rise to crime and criminals must be destroyed. We won't achieve these goals by suppressing the man who, rather than die a slow death caused by the privations he had and will have to put up with without any hope of ever seeing them end, prefers—if he has the least bit of energy—to violently take what can ensure his well-being, even at the risk of death, which would only put an end to his sufferings.

So that is why I committed the acts of which I am accused, and which are nothing but the logical consequence of the barbaric state of a society that does nothing but increase the rigor of the laws that pursue the effects without ever touching the causes. It is said that you must be cruel to kill your fellow man, but those who say this don't see that you resolve to do this only to avoid the same fate.

In the same way you, gentlemen of the jury, will doubtless sentence me to death, because you think it is necessary and that my death will be a source of satisfaction for you who hate to see human blood flow. But when you think it is useful to have it flow in order to ensure the security of your existence you hesitate no more than

I do, but with this difference: you do it without running any risk, while I, on the other hand, acted at the risk of my very life.

Well, messieurs, there are no more criminals to judge, but the causes of crime to do away with! In creating the articles of the Criminal Code, the legislators forgot that they didn't attack the causes, but only the effects, and so they don't in any way destroy crime. In truth, the causes continuing to exist, the effects will necessarily flow from them. There will always be criminals, for today you destroy one, but tomorrow ten will be born.

What, then, is needed? Destroy poverty, that seed of crime, by assuring everyone the satisfaction of their needs! How difficult this is to realize! All that is needed is to establish society on a new basis, where everything will be held in common and where each, producing according to his abilities and his strength, could consume according to his needs. Then and only then will we no longer see people such as the hermit of Notre-Dame-de-Grâce and others, begging for a metal whose victims and slaves they become! We will no longer see women surrendering their charms, like a common piece of merchandise, in exchange for this same metal that often prevents us from recognizing whether or not affection is sincere. We will no longer see men such as Pranzini, Prado, Berland, Anastay,[1] and others who kill in order to have this same metal. This shows that the cause of all crimes is always the same, and you have to be foolish not to see this.

Yes, I repeat it: it is society that makes criminals and you, gentlemen of the jury, instead of striking you should

---

1 Famous criminals of the late 1880s and early 1890s. All were executed.

use your intelligence and your strength to transform society. In one fell swoop you'll suppress all crime. And your work, in attacking causes, will be greater and more fruitful than your justice, which belittles itself in punishing its effects.

I am nothing but an uneducated worker; but because I have lived the life of the poor, I feel more than a rich bourgeois does the iniquity of your repressive laws. What gives you the right to kill or lock up a man who, put on earth with the need to live, found himself obliged to take that which he lacks in order to feed himself?

I worked to live and to provide for my family; as long as neither I nor my family suffered too much, I remained what you call honest. Then work became scarce, and with unemployment came hunger. It is only then that the great law of nature, that imperious voice that accepts no reply, the instinct of preservation, forced me to commit some of the crimes and misdemeanors of which I am accused and of which I admit I am the author.

Judge me, gentlemen of the jury, but if you have understood me, while judging *me* judge all the unfortunate who poverty, combined with natural pride, made criminals, and who wealth or ease would have made honest men.

An intelligent society would have made of them men like any other!

My Principles

Editor's note: Ravachol dictated this document to the police while in prison. It remained unpublished until the historian Jean Maitron found it in the Paris Police Archives in 1964.

The above named, after having eaten his fill, spoke to us as follows:

"Messieurs, it is my habit, wherever I am, to do propaganda work. Do you know what anarchism is?"

We answered "No" to this question.

"This doesn't surprise me," he responded. "The working class, which, like you, is forced to work to earn its bread, doesn't have the time to devote to the reading of pamphlets they're given. It's the same for you.

"Anarchy is the obliteration of property. There currently exist many useless things; many occupations are useless as well, for example, accounting. With anarchy there is no more need for money, no further need for bookkeeping and the other forms of employment that derive from this. There are currently too many citizens who suffer while others swim in opulence, in abundance. This situation cannot last; we all should profit by the surplus of the rich; but even more obtain, like them, all [of] which is necessary. In current society it isn't possible to reach this goal. Nothing, not even a tax on income, could change the face of things. Nevertheless, the bulk of workers think that if we acted in this way, things would improve. It is an error to think this way. If we tax the landlord, he'll increase his rents and in this way he will arrange for those who suffer to pay the new charges imposed on them. In any event, no law can touch landlords for, being the masters of their goods, we can't prevent them from doing whatever they want with them. What, then, should be done? Wipe out property and, by doing this, wipe out those who take all. If this abolition takes place we have to also do away with money in order to prevent any idea of accumulation, which would force a return to the current regime. It is in fact money that is the cause of all discord, all hatred, all ambitions; it is, in a word, the creator of property. This metal, in truth, has nothing but an agreed-upon price, born of its rarity. If we were no longer obliged to give something in exchange for those things we need to live, gold would lose its value and no one would seek it. Nor could they enrich themselves, because nothing they would amass could serve them in obtaining a life better than that of others. There would then no longer be any need of laws, no need of masters.

"As for religions, they'd be destroyed, because their moral influence would no longer have any reason to exist. There would no longer be the absurdity of believing in a God who doesn't exist, since after death everything is finished. So we should hold fast to life. But when I say life I mean life, which does not mean slaving all day to make the bosses fat and, while dying oneself of hunger, become the authors of their well-being.

"Masters aren't necessary, these people whose idleness is maintained by our labor; everyone must make himself useful to society, by which I mean work according to his ability and his aptitude. In this way, one would be a baker, another a teacher, etc. Following this principle, work would decrease and each of us would have only an hour or two of work a day. Man, not being able to remain without some form of occupation, would find his distraction in work; there would be no lazy idlers, and if they did exist, there'd be so few of them that we could leave them in peace and, without complaint, let them profit from the work of others.

"There being no more laws, marriage would be destroyed. We would unite by inclination, and the family would be founded on the love of a father and mother for their children. For example, if a woman no longer loved the man whom she had chosen as a companion, she could separate from him and form a new association. In a word, complete freedom to live with those we love. If in the case I just cited there were children, society would raise them, that is to say, those who will love the children will take them in charge.

"With this free union, there will be no more prostitution. Secret illnesses would no longer exist, since these are only born of the abuse of the coming together of the sexes; an abuse to which women are forced to submit, since society's current conditions oblige them to take this up as a job in order to survive. Isn't money necessary in order to live, earned at whatever cost?

"With my principles, which I can't in so little time lay out in full detail, the army will no longer have any reason to exist, since there will no longer be distinct nations; private property would be destroyed, and all nations would have joined into one, which would be the Universe.

"No more war, no more disputes, no more jealousy, no more theft, no more murder, no more court system, no more police, no more administration.

"The anarchists have not yet gone into the details of their constitution: the mileposts alone have been laid out.

Today the anarchists are numerous enough to overthrow the current state of things, and if that hasn't yet happened, it's because we must complete the education of the followers, give birth in them to the energy and the firm will to assist in the realization of their projects. All that is needed for that is a shove, that someone put himself at their head, and the revolution will take place.

"The man who blows up houses has as his goal the extermination of all those who, by their social standing or their acts, are harmful to anarchy. If it was permitted to openly attack these people without fearing for the police, and so for one's skin, we wouldn't set out to destroy their homes though explosive devices, which could kill the suffering classes they have at their service at the same time as them."

Liberté, Égalité, Fraternité

Editor's note: For a period in the 1880s, Ravachol earned his living as a musician. A contemporary passed down the lyrics to one of his songs.

Children of the same fatherland
Can't you hear the voice
That cries out for democracy.
To arms against the bourgeoisie.
Let's fight for independence
And for sacred liberty,
Through the efforts of our might
Let's transform society.
Why, on this earth,
Do we betray ourselves
When we should love each other as brothers?
Our masters cause disunion;
Let's drive out authoritarian chiefs
Full of hatred and iniquity.
Peoples, let's put an end to borders
To the cry of "Long Live Equality!"
In order to establish equality
You need a heart full of hate.
Reduce the bourgeoisie to dust
Then instead of war
We'll have brotherhood.

■ FOR RAVACHOL

La Ravachole

Editor's note: Sung to the tune of the song of the French Revolution, La Carmagnole—*the chorus of which ends "Long live the sound of the cannon"—*La Ravachole *set the spirit of the anarchist Ravachol to music.*

In the great city of Paris,
There are well-fed bourgeois,
There are the poor,
Who have an empty stomach:
The former are greedy,
Long live the sound, long live the sound,
The former are greedy,
Long live the sound
Of the explosion!

Let's dance the Ravachole
Long live the sound, long live the sound
Let's dance the Ravachole
Of the explosion!

Ah ça ira ça ira ça ira
All the bourgeois will taste the bomb
Ah ça ira ça ira ça ira
We'll blow up all the bourgeois
We'll blow them up!

There are sellout magistrates,
There are big-bellied financiers,
There are cops,
But for all these scoundrels,
There's dynamite,
Long live the sound, long live the sound,
There's dynamite,
Long live the sound,
Of the explosion!

There are the feeble-minded senators,
There are the rotten deputies,
There are the generals,
Murderers, and executioners,
Butchers in uniform,
Long live the sound, long live the sound,
Butchers in uniform,
Long live the sound
Of the explosion!

. . .

Ah, goddammit, it's time to put an end to this,
We've moaned and suffered long enough,
No halfway war,
No more cowardly pity,

Death to the bourgeoisie!
Long live the sound, long live the sound
Death to the bourgeoisie!
Long live the sound
Of the explosion!

Eulogy for Ravachol
By Paul Adam

Editor's note: Paul Adam (1862–1920) was a writer and critic who, after his anarchist beginnings, eventually became an extreme nationalist.

Miracles and saints seem to have vanished in our time. It could be easily believed that contemporary souls lacked the spirit of sacrifice. The martyrs of this century were usually obscure citizens made mad by the din of political speech, and who were then mercilessly gunned down in 1830, 1848, and 1871 so that violent and shifty lawyers could obtain the parliamentary posts that they had prepared for themselves. And it would be imprudent to say that these unfortunate combatants weren't driven by private interest to themselves seek some electoral profit, weapon in hand.

The spectacle of the two Chambers, with their daily scandals, their syndicates of sugar manufacturers, boilers of vintages, beer sellers, winemakers, grain brokers, and cattle raisers, has often revealed the real reasons behind universal suffrage. There was Marie Reynard and Wilson, Méline and Morelli, Senator Le Guay . . . And so all those street battles in Paris, those stories of the Rue Transnonain and Satory,[1] ended as simple quarrels between competing merchants.

Our souls lacking in complexity would probably have stopped following the games of these marionettes, and

---

1 A group of antigovernment protestors was murdered on the Rue Transnonain in Paris in 1834. Communards were imprisoned at the camp of Satory, and a group of leaders of the Commune was executed there.

politics would have stopped interesting us if the legend of sacrifice, of the giving of a life for human happiness, hadn't suddenly reappeared in our era with Ravachol's martyrdom.

Whatever the invective of the bourgeois press and the tenacity of the magistrates in condemning the vctim's act, they didn't succeed in convincing us of his falseness. After so many judicial debates, articles, and appeals for legal murder, Ravachol remains the propagator of the grand ideas of the ancient religions, which advocated the seeking of individual death for the good of the world; the abnegation of the self, of one's life and renown for the exaltation of the poor, of the humble. He is irrevocably the Renewer of the Essential Sacrifice.

Asserting his right to exist at the risk of allowing himself to be held in contempt by the herd of civic slaves; risking the ignominy of the scaffold; conceiving the technique of suppressing the useless in order to support an idea of liberation; having the boldness to conceive and the devotion to accomplish this: is all this not enough to merit the title of Redeemer?

Of all of Ravachol's acts there is one that is perhaps the most symbolic. In opening the grave of the old woman and blindly searching for the jewel on the sticky hands of the corpse, a jewel capable of saving a poor family from hunger for a month, he demonstrated the shame of a society that sumptuously decorates its carrion while in just one year ninety-one thousand individuals die of hunger within the frontiers of the wealthy country of France without anyone even thinking about it, aside from him and us.

The act was even more significant because his attempt was futile and the corpse was lacking in finery. His act was stripped of any real profit and takes on the abstract allure of a logical and deductive idea. From the affirmation that nothing should belong to someone with no immediate need of it, it is proven that every need must find satisfaction. This is Christ's formula, to each according to his needs, so marvelously translated in the parable of the father who pays at the same price the workers who went to his vineyard at dawn, those who went at noon, and those hired in the evening. Work doesn't merit wages, but needs must be satisfied. You shouldn't give in the hope of remunerative recognition, or for a labor useful to you, but solely from love of your fellow man, to quench your hunger for altruism, your thirst for the good and the beautiful, your passion for harmony and universal happiness.

If Ravachol is condemned for the murder of the hermit, can't he find arguments in his defense every day in the *faits divers* in the papers? Is he guiltier than society, which allows beings to perish in the solitude of garrets people as useful as the student at the École des Beaux-Arts recently found dead in Paris for want of bread? Society kills more than assassins do; and when a man driven to the most horrific poverty arms his despair and strikes in order not to succumb, is he not the legitimate defender of a life with which, in an instant of pleasure, his unthinking parents charged him? As long as there exist men who slowly suffer from hunger until their final exhaustion, theft and murder will remain natural. No form of justice can logically oppose this idea and punish unless it faithfully and unambiguously declares itself to be force-crushing weakness. But if a new force rises up to confront it, it should not condemn the enemy. It must accept the duel and handle the enemy gingerly, so that when it is defeated it will find the New Force clement.

Ravachol was the champion of this New Force. He was the first to lay out the theories of his acts and the logic of his crimes, and no public declamation is capable of convicting him of misguided ways or errors. His act is the consequence of his ideas and his ideas are born of the barbarism in which pitiful humanity vegetates.

Ravachol saw suffering all around him, and he exalted the sffering of others in offering his own in a holocaust. His charity, his disinterestedness, the vigor of his acts, his courage in the face of irremediable death elevate him to the splendors of legend. In these times of cynicism and irony, a saint has been born to us.

His blood shall be the example that new brave men and new martyrs shall drink. The great idea of universal altruism will flourish in the red puddle that will soon lie pooled at the foot of the guillotine.

A fertile death will soon occur. An epoch in human history will be marked in the annals of the people. The legal murder of Ravachol will open an era.

And you artists who, with a talkative brush, recount on your canvases your mystical dreams, are offered here a great subject. If you've understood your epoch, if you've recognized and kissed the doorway to the future, it is up to you to trace the life and passing of this saint in a pious triptych. For a time will come when in the temples of Real Fraternity your stained glass will be placed in the most beautiful spot so that the light of the sun, passing through the halo of the martyr, can illuminate the gratitude of men free of egoism on a planet free of property.

From *Entretiens Politiques et Littéraires*, July 28, 1892.

Guillotinade
By Émile Pouget

Editor's note: Émile Pouget (1860–1931) founded and edited the newspaper Le Père Peinard, *written in working-class slang. He advocated sabotage and the general strike.*

"I hope that the members of the jury, in sentencing me to death, casting into despair those who still have affection for me, carry on their consciences the memory of their sentence with as much lightness and courage as I will carry my head under the blade of the guillotine."

Those were Ravachol's last words after his sentencing.

And goddammit, it's that very calm that the jackasses who sent him to his death have not yet found.

The mere idea of cutting the guy's head off scares the shit out of the governmental brigands. Even so, it's already three quarters done: all that's left to do is push the button on Deibler's machine.[2]

But they find this as hard to pull off as if they had the whole trial to do over again.

They're uneasy, those cowards. They're afraid that a vengeance that's in the air will descend on the guillotine and on them.

And so they really want to get this thing done. Hoping to find calm after the murder, they're moving up the day. Maybe it's already been done.

How many precautions they're taking for this murder.

---

2 Louis Deibler (1823–1904), public executioner of France.

34

The jackasses have filled Montbrison with soldiers.[3] They've mobilized all the cops and squealers of France.

Gendarmes, old soldiers, cops in uniform and out, they've been scattered all over the place. All along the roads, under every paving stone.

All this because the guillotining of Ravachol isn't something ordinary, it's not the execution of a man: he's the first anarchist guillotined in France!

And this is something serious, goddammit!

This is what leads the government bandits to hesitate.

In fact, it's not just a matter of the pissing of Ravachol's blood.

It has to be digested.

Won't it curdle on the conscience of the bourgeois?

Won't it suffocate the jackasses?

This is what the future will tell us, goddammit!

From *Le Père Peinard* 173, July 10–17, 1892.

---

3 Montbrison was the prison where Ravachol's execution took place.

Ravachol's Laugh
By Victor Barrucand

Editor's note: Victor Barrucand (1864–1934) was an anarchist writer, poet, and playwright, and one of the driving forces in the movement for the provision of free bread to the poor.

The anarchist's head has fallen beneath the legal knife to the applause of a cowardly and complicit society. Ravachol is dead, an insult on his lips, ironic and contemptuous, dominating the vile crowd with his disdain. Never faltering, he scoffed with his tragic laugh those who stabbed themselves with the two-edged sword they had used to defend themselves. And moral victory is his in the minds of those who view things clearly, outside the prejudices of a police-run civilization.

Oh, that laugh before the sinister machine—Homeric derision reverberating in the silence of a summer morn, where all of life wanted to smile—sends a funereal chill up our spines. And the social whore at the base of the scaffold, struck by the sarcasm and defiance of a criminal who cares not at all for politesse and who acts with an amazing energy, has been condemned for all eternity, as if all her infamies and irremediable mediocrity had been thrown in her face in the spittle she so richly deserved.

His blasphemous mockery immutably fixed in the rictus of death, the head of the rebel, beautiful and purified, with its legendary authority, remains. Eloquent and worthy of love because of the poverty in which he lived, the ignominy he suffered, it radiates a fascination for the weak for whom it provides comfort. With the prestige of interpretations and the miracle of haughty sympathies, Ravachol will perhaps someday appear a violent Christ, the kind his time and milieu was able to produce, and not all that much inferior to desirable ideals. He will perhaps be compared to that other torture victim, Jesus the Galilean, who in certain ways was an anarchist, as Ernest Renan has noted.

Both of them, these demolishers of the temple, wanted to do away with wealth and power, but not in order to take them for themselves. One preached gentleness, the spirit of sacrifice and renunciation, freedom from political hindrances through disdain with the goal of conquering the celestial kingdom. The other preached by example revolt against abusive authority, individual initiative against the cowardice of the masses, the demand of the poor for happiness on earth. Freed from narrow egoism, they gained greater awareness of themselves as part of humanity. Despite apparent differences between them, setting out from the principle of love they marched toward their goal. With heroic will they taught the world that the ideas of fatherland and society, no more than those of religion and the law, can prevail against man's right to be happy. In this world, Ravachol said; in heaven, said Jesus.

Even if the pursuit of this parallel offered a paradoxical interest, there are nevertheless curious coincidences: the age of thirty-three at which they both died and the traitor who turned them in with a kiss, Chaumartin[4] filling in for Judas Iscariot.

---

4 Acquitted co-defendant in Ravachol's anarchist trial who had turned informant.

The possibility of such a comparison, and the idea that the victim of Montbrison could spread a salutary contagion through the example of his life and his death, a new morality without obligation or sanction that would abrogate the ancient law; these are the consequences that would make smile those who believe they possess the true truth outside of which there is no salvation. But those who recognize the emptiness of absolutes and know that the future belongs to inflexible wills will not be tempted to respond with a shrug and a smug smile to Ravachol's laugh, bitterer and stronger than that of Voltaire, that other demolisher.

From *L'Endehors* 64, July 24, 1892.

The Little Ravachols Will Grow Up
By Gustave Mathieu

Editor's note: An article by Gustave Mathieu, a friend and an accomplice of the anarchist hero, written shortly before Ravachol's execution in 1892. Here, he makes a clear connection between Ravachol the criminal and Ravachol the anarchist.

After all the misadventures of the policemen trailing me and the reporters pursuing me, and in memory of the interest they've always shown me, I perhaps owe them an update. This is an occasion for me to offer my fraternal hand to the friend who I haven't forgotten.

If I'm writing these lines it's not to defend Ravachol as a martyr: in the cause for which we fight—sincere, convinced, and without let-up—there are no martyrs. Rather than wasting away in a capitalist prison camp, sweating, toiling in order to enrich the exploiters, succumbing to privations and poorly paid work, isn't it better to act like a revolutionary?

Can it be said that Ravachol wasn't called upon to know this sad existence? On the contrary, from an early age he had to work to bring a meager mouthful to his brothers and sisters, brought up in poverty by a mother who had remained a widow.

Of a sickly temperament, and seeing that despite working like a slave his family's poverty only grew worse, he reflected . . . and he said that rather than suffer like a resigned slave it would be better to take their stolen riches from the exploiters.

He often said: No luxury, only what is necessary. Enough of this life of flabbiness and moral degradation. Dignity, courage, and, at the risk of our own lives, let us kill all the exploiters of the world.

Alas, the results of individual propaganda are paid for in a horrible fashion.

Which is what happened to my friend.

Ravachol held his head high before the lackeys of the magistracy, taking responsibility for his acts, declaring that in our sad society the life of the workers is a hell.

How ironic it is to give all your strength when you're young and to see yourself rejected everywhere when you're old!

You have no right to call yourself an anarchist. You're nothing but a murderer, the cloaked ones answered.

And what are you, you who judge?

The fences of bandits who starve the poor, and of the Lavassiès of all the *Comptoirs d'escompte*; repulsive beings who approve the idleness of rich playboys and the shooting down of workers, like those of Fourmies,[5] beggars who disturb your digestion. This is what you call order. So be it. You are playing your role, you have force behind you, and taking advantage of this you condemned Ravachol to death.

Perhaps you think that, like in the Anstay case, we're going to call for an autopsy of our friend in order to prove that he wasn't responsible for his acts. Not at all! Ravachol had a healthy mind and a proud heart when he took the money he needed to live wherever he found it, money useful for propaganda. The hermit of Chambles made

5 The site where nine eight-hour-day demonstrators were killed on May 1, 1889. At the subsequent trial, demonstrators were sent to prison.

possible the Rue de Clichy. Ravachol's entire existence followed the logic of the rebel.

And you can kill him, but you'll never be able to stifle the voice of the rebels: the little Ravachols will grow up. You can do what you want, but they'll be more adroit and terrible than their predecessor.

Furthermore, the execution will be a challenge thrown at the anarchists, a challenge that will fall into good hands. The bourgeois press can slander as much as it wants, invent incredible lies, such as the kidnapping of the bourgeois Deibler.[6] Let it beware that reality doesn't one day go beyond its predictions.

The squealer Véry,[7] who was so carefully guarded, better even than Deibler now is, nevertheless paid for his denunciation.

If Deibler hasn't yet thought about retiring, I think for his own safety it would be prudent to impose it on him.

From *L'Endehors* 61, July 3, 1892.

---

6 The public executioner.

7 Véry was the owner of the restaurant that bore his name that was bombed in retaliation for Ravachol's arrest; he died in the explosion. The actual informant was the waiter, Lherot.

■ AUGUSTE VAILLANT

The Interrogation of Vaillant

It was exactly 9:00 a.m. when Messieurs Lepine, police prefect; Roulier, *procureur* of the Republic; Clément, judicial commissioner; Meyer, investigating magistrate; and Fedée, police officer, went to the Hôtel-Dieu Hospital for the interrogation of Vaillant, alias Marchal.

The wounded man was lying on his bed, his cut face bearing a cloth band compressing the light wound on his nose. He didn't appear in the least perturbed by the magistrates' entrance into the small room where he was being held. He raised himself slightly on his elbow and stretched his neck in a movement of expectation and cheeky curiosity.

The investigating magistrate Meyer having asked him if his condition allowed him to bear a long interrogation Vaillant dryly responded: "Perfectly." His face then lit up with a strange, mocking, almost demonic smile.

"Until now," M. Meyer said to him, "you've had a strange attitude that seems to confirm the suspicions against you. The information gathered about you presents you as a man particularly devoted to anarchism."

"Indeed I am an anarchist and I am proud of it."

"What did you go to do at the Chamber yesterday?"

"I went there to do what pleased me. There were many others besides me."

"Why these two names, Marchal and Vaillant, which you gave in different places?"

"Because it pleased me to act that way. I have no explanations to give you."

"But you had a goal in seeking to hide your identity."

"A goal? Not at all. My name is Vaillant in Choisy-le-Roi and Marchal in Paris. There are tons of people who have pseudonyms. What does that prove?"

"It proves you are a suspect."

Vaillant interrupted the judge with a loud laugh.

"So I'm a suspect," he shouted with his loud, metallic voice. "Suspected of what? Of having thrown the bomb in the Chamber of Deputies? That's why you've come here to interrogate me, why you're nosing around trying to get answers out of me. There's no need to work so hard at this."

And Vaillant added, shaking his head with an air of satisfaction and defiance:

"Well, I'm the one who did it. It's unfortunate that it's some sad buggers who are taking the rap. I'd have loved to make a fricassee of those deputy bastards."

"What had the deputies ever done to you?"

"What did they do to me? To me personally, nothing. But they're people it wouldn't be such a bad thing to be rid of."

"And you committed this odious act without thinking that you have a wife and children?"

"Oh my wife and children won't be any worse off when they don't have me than when they do."

Vaillant then complacently provided the information that was asked of him about his past. He was born in Mézières December 29, 1861, and he worked at various professions. His last position was at the leather craft store of M. Petitpoint in Choisy-le-Roi.

The idea to throw the bomb at the Chamber came to Vaillant after the rejection of the proposed amnesty bill. Well before this the anarchist had developed a plan to commit an attack in Paris "to frighten the bourgeois," but this plan was still quite vague and he didn't know whom he'd attack. Auguste Vaillant left his home in Choisy-le-Roi on November 26, leaving in distress his mistress Marchal and a little girl named Sidonie, whom he'd had with his legitimate spouse, currently in America.[1] He went to Paris and moved in to 70 Rue Daguerre in a hotel owned by Mme Picard. He arrived at this establishment, one of a low order, on November 27, his baggage consisting of only a valise in bad condition and a blackened wooden box with crude hinges and a primitive lock. For the sum of twenty-four francs per month, he rented room two, on the second floor on the street side.

The existence Vaillant led in this tiny room was extremely mysterious: he never received any guests but he often went out at night, often not returning. Nevertheless, he enjoyed a certain amount of consideration in the hotel, where he was registered under the name Marchal. As proof of identity he had provided the owner a marriage license in this name, which we know to be that of his mistress. The latter must have been or must be married. He inspired confidence by paying a month in advance. But he never

---

1 Actually in Argentina.

went out without taking his valise and only wanted his room done in his presence.

On the eve of the attack, that is Friday, Vaillant returned home at noon, lay down, and then went out again at about six. He asked Mme Picard for the address of a locksmith to repair his cloth bag, one of whose hinges he said was broken. The hotel keeper gave him the address of a locksmith on the Rue Gassendi, who wasn't in when the anarchist went there.

After that no one saw Vaillant; he refused to say where he spent the night of Friday into Saturday in order "not to compromise a comrade."

The accused gave all this information with good grace, all the while smiling, mockingly affirming its scrupulous accuracy.

Nor did he hesitate to give a complete description of the murderous device that he made with his own hands. The examination of the metal debris found in the Chamber had led people to believe that the explosive was contained in a soldier's can or in a mess tin. It is Vaillant himself who said he used a worker's canteen, that is, a tin recipient fifteen centimeters high and oval in form. This utensil usually has a cap and a handle used for carrying it. In order for the bomb to take up as little room as possible in his pocket Vaillant removed the handle, one of the fasteners, as well as the cap. He obtained this object and one like it at the Bazaar of the Hôtel de Ville.

The explosive used in the improvised bomb was made of chlorate powder and the projectiles, as we already know, were simple cobblers' nails. In the middle Vaillant had placed a glass ampoule filled with sulfuric acid whose extremity was formed by a cotton tampon. The device was of the type known as a reversal device. Once the canteen was turned upside down the acid ate away at the tampon and the contact of the acid with the powder charge caused the latter to be set alight.

It is believed that Vaillant used 750 grams of nails.

The anarchist admits that he himself manipulated the substances that made up the chlorate powder but he refuses to say how he obtained these products. Nor did he want to divulge the address of the nail merchant.

"How did you enter the Chamber?" they then asked the anarchist.

"Easily. With a card given me by M. Argeliès, deputy from the Seine-et-Oise."

"And how did you throw your bomb?"

"I was seated in the second row of the spectators, against the barrier of the gallery reserved for members of the public with tickets. I had my bomb in the right-hand pocket of my overcoat and I held myself perfectly still in order to avoid a shock that would have produced a premature explosion. I waited an hour for the favorable moment to throw my box and took advantage of the moment when the deputies' attention was concentrated on the gallery, where M. Mirman had just spoken. My intention was to throw my device so that it fell in the hemicycle at the foot of the gallery. But a lady sitting next to me prevented me from fully extending my arm and I wasn't able to throw the bomb as vigorously as I would have liked. The bomb exploded in the air and I was one of the first victims of the explosion."

"What did you do afterward?"

"I sought to flee. I went downstairs, wiping the blood dripping from my nose with a handkerchief, and I found the doors closed, which didn't surprise me at all, since I'd heard the order given by M. Bizarelli."

"And afterward?"

"Afterward I went back up, crossing the rotunda. I walked through the corridors of the galleries and then went to the urinals. Someone said to me, 'You're wounded, go get yourself taken care of at the infirmary.' After my head was wrapped in a bandage the police grabbed me and took me to a superintendent. You know the rest."

He was asked if he regretted his act and Vaillant responded: "I regret nothing at all, and if I was free I'd do it all over again. The people have been suffering for long enough. All methods are good to hasten their deliverance."

And Vaillant added with a tone of profound conviction:

"I'm proud of the act I committed. If you think I had accomplices you're wrong. I did all this on my own, and if my spontaneous confession gives me the right to a favor I ask you to bother no one because of me."

From *Le Matin*, December 11, 1893.

Vaillant's Courtroom Speech

Gentlemen, in a few minutes you are to deal your blow, but in receiving your verdict I shall at least have the satisfaction of having injured the existing society, this cursed society in which one may see a single man uselessly spending enough to feed thousands of families; an infamous society that permits a few individuals to monopolize all social wealth, while there are hundreds of thousands of unfortunates who have not even the bread that is not refused to dogs, and while entire families are committing suicide for want of the necessities of life.

Ah, gentlemen, if the governing classes could go down among the unfortunates! But no, they prefer to remain deaf to their appeals. It seems that a fatality impels them, like the royalty of the eighteenth century, toward the precipice that will engulf them, for woe on those who remain deaf to the cries of the starving, woe on those who, believing themselves of superior essence, assume the right to exploit those beneath them! There comes a time when the people no longer reason; they rise like a hurricane, and pass away like a torrent. Then we see bleeding heads impaled on pikes.

Among the exploited, gentlemen, there are two classes of individuals. Those of one class, not realizing what they are and what they might be, take life as it comes, believe that they are born to be slaves, and content themselves with the little that is given them in exchange for their labor. But there are others, on the contrary, who think, who study, and who, looking about them, discover social iniquities. Is it their fault if they see clearly and suffer at seeing others suffer? Then they throw themselves into the struggle, and make themselves the bearers of the popular claims.

Gentlemen, I am one of the latter. Wherever I have gone, I have seen unfortunates bent beneath the yoke of capital. Everywhere I have seen the same wounds causing tears of blood to flow, even in the remoter parts of the inhabited districts of South America, where I had the right to believe that he who was weary of the pains of civilization might rest in the shade of the palm trees and there study nature. Well, there even, more than elsewhere, I have seen capital come, like a vampire, to suck the last drop of blood of the unfortunate pariahs.

Then I came back to France, where I was forced to see my family suffer atrociously. This was the last drop in the cup of my sorrow. Tired of leading this life of suffering and cowardice, I carried this bomb to those who are primarily responsible for social misery.

I am reproached with the wounds of those who were struck by my projectiles. Permit me to point out in passing that, if the bourgeois had not massacred or caused massacres during the Revolution, it is probable that they would still be under the yoke of the nobility. On the other hand, figure up the dead and wounded in Tonkin, Madagascar, Dahomey, adding to this the thousands, yes, millions of unfortunates who die in the factories, the mines, and wherever the grinding power of capital is felt. Add also those who die of hunger, and all this with the assent of our Deputies. Beside all this, of how little weight are the reproaches now brought against me!

It is true that one does not efface the other; but, after all, are we not acting on the defensive when we respond to the blows that we receive from above? I know very well that I shall be told that I ought to have confined myself to speech for the vindication of the people's claims. But what can you expect! It takes a loud voice to make the deaf hear. Too long have they answered our voices by imprisonment, the rope, and rifle volleys. Make no mistake; the explosion of my bomb is not only the cry of the rebel Vaillant, but the cry of an entire class that vindicates its rights, and that will soon add acts to words. For, be sure of it, in vain will they pass laws. The ideas of the thinkers will not halt. Just as, in the last century, all the governmental forces could not prevent the Diderots and the Voltaires from spreading emancipating ideas among the people, so all the existing governmental forces will not prevent the Reclus, the Darwins, the Spencers, the Ibsens, the Mirbeaus from spreading the ideas of justice and liberty that will annihilate the prejudices that hold the mass in ignorance. And these ideas, welcomed by the unfortunate, will flower in acts of revolt as they have done in me, until the day when the disappearance of authority shall permit all men to organize freely according to their choice, when everyone shall be able to enjoy the product of his labor, and when those moral maladies called prejudices shall vanish, permitting human beings to live in harmony, having no other desire than to study the sciences and love their fellows.

I conclude, gentlemen, by saying that a society in which one sees such social inequalities as we see all about us, in which we every day see suicides caused by poverty, prostitution flaring at every street corner, a society whose principal monuments are barracks and prisons: such a society must be transformed as soon as possible, on pain of being eliminated, and that speedily, from the human race. Hail to him who labors, by no matter what means, for this transformation! It is this idea that has guided me in my duel with authority, but as in this duel I have only wounded my adversary, it is now its turn to strike me.

Now, gentlemen, to me it matters little what penalty you may inflict, for, looking at this assembly with the eyes of reason, I cannot help smiling to see you, atoms lost in matter, and reasoning only because you possess a prolongation of the spinal marrow, assume the right to judge one of your fellows.

Ah! gentlemen, how small a thing is your assembly and your verdict in the history of humanity; and human history, in its turn, is likewise a very little thing in the whirlwind that bears it through immensity, and that is destined to disappear, or at least to be transformed, in order to begin again the same history and the same facts, a veritably perpetual play of cosmic forces renewing and transferring themselves forever.

■ ÉMILE HENRY

Émile Henry's Indictment

The accused was born in Spain where his parents took refuge after the events of 1871, in which they'd taken an active part.

In 1882, after the amnesty, his parents returned to France.

He received a complete education, presented for the entrance examination for the École Polytechnique, but failed the second part of the test. He then entered the shop of a construction engineer, who sent him to Venice to work on a public works project for which he was the contractor. Barely three months later he left a job that could have been a career.

When he returned to Paris he found himself at a commercial establishment that paid him 125 francs per month. At that time he became, to use his own words, a determined anarchist. The superiority of his education led him to acquire in a very short time a certain notoriety among the "companions." On May 31, 1892, following the first anarchist attacks, he was arrested but was soon set free.

Shortly afterward his boss, who saw him making propaganda among his comrades, decided to fire him. After his departure he [the boss] found in his [Henry's] desk manuscripts relating to the fabrication of explosives and a manual called "Practical Anarchism" that began with these words: "We ask the companions to execute these works."

After having collaborated for a time at the offices of *L'Endehors* the accused worked as a clerk at the home of the sculptor-decorator Dupuis.

Two days after the explosion on the Rue des Bons-Enfants he disappeared. Despite this striking coincidence he denies having participated in this attack: He said that he was then in England, fearing he'd be arrested again."

His trail is lost from that time until last December 20. On that date he presented himself at the Villa Faucheur, Rue des Envierges, and rented a room under the name Louis Dubois.

There he obtained the materials needed for the making of explosive devices, notably picric acid, and busied himself with preparing a bomb.

In a small metal kettle, whose handle he removed, as well as the button on the cover, he placed a cylindrical zinc envelope.

He declared that between this envelope and the flared wall of the kettle he placed 121 gun balls.

Inside the zinc cylinder he placed another, smaller, one, filling the space between them with an explosive substance.

Finally, in the smallest one he placed a dynamite cartridge with a primer made of fulminate of mercury. Against this primer he placed a miner's fuse calculated to burn fifteen seconds.

On February 2, he left his room after having warned the guardian of the villa that he wouldn't be home for a few days. According to his declaration he left three and a half kilos of picric acid there. He carried his bomb, following Vaillant's example, in his belt.

He had a loaded revolver whose cartridges he'd chewed in order, he said, to do more harm, and a dagger whose blade he'd sought to poison.

Armed in this way he headed toward the Avenue de l'Opéra, took a look at the Bignon Restaurant, then the Café Américain, then the Café de la Paix, but he didn't find a sufficient number of victims in any of them and continued on his way.

At the Café Terminus, where he arrived at about eight thirty, the crowd was especially dense around a platform where an orchestra was playing.

He entered, sat down at a table near the door, and asked for a beer, which he paid for in advance.

He soon had a second one served along with a cigar, which he also paid for as soon as they were brought. He waited for the crowd to grow larger.

At nine, he approached his lit cigar to the end of the fuse, got up, and reached the door, which was only a short distance away.

He then turned around and threw the bomb in the direction of the orchestra.

The device struck the electric lights, broke one of the crystal tulips, and fell to the ground, spreading a thick and acrid smoke.

A few seconds later, it exploded with a muffled detonation, caving in the floor and wounding seventeen people.

The assassin fled, shouting, "Oh the wretch, where is he?"

He was immediately pursued by the waiter Tissier and by two customers who'd seen him throw the device.

The guardian of the peace Poisson, who was stationed in the guardhouse across from the café, also ran after him.

At the corner of the Rue de Havre and the Rue d'Isly, an employee of the Compagnie de l'Ouest, M. Etienne, caught up with him and put his hand on his shoulder saying, "I have you, you scoundrel!" "Not yet," answered the accused, who shot him in the chest.

Fortunately the ball flattened against a button and didn't penetrate, but Etienne fell in a faint.

M. Maurice, a coiffeur, then grabbed him a little further away. A second shot threw him to the ground, giving him a serious wound.

The agent Poisson then arrived. The accused aimed at him but missed and he continued along his route. Poisson drew his saber and continued his pursuit. He had almost caught up with him when a shot hit him in the chest. He remained standing and raised his arms in order to strike, and the accused fired the two last shots of his revolver. One of the balls struck his right side and the other was lost in the policeman's wallet.

The latter jumped on the accused and they fell to the ground together.

Other agents arrived at the moment Poisson lost consciousness. They took hold of Henry, whom they had to protect against the anger of the crowd.

During the course of his questioning Henry, who had at first taken the false name of Breton, showed no regret for the series of criminal acts.

On the contrary, in front of one of his victims, M. Etienne, he expressed regret at having used a defective revolver as well as for having decreased the explosive force of his bomb by poorly attaching the cover of the kettle.

The expert brought in by the investigating magistrate declared that the device thrown by Henry was "combined and constructed in a manner to kill upon falling in the midst of a crowd and to partially destroy the building in which it would be thrown."

Like all anarchists, he declared that he acted under the influence of a purely personal resolution.

Nevertheless, if the investigation didn't establish any act of legal complicity, it nevertheless showed that other anarchists knew his plans.

In fact, on the morning of February 14, the guardian of the Villa Faucheur remarked that the door of Henry's room had been broken open.

The police superintendent, called to the room, discovered a miner's fuse, lead balls, and a quantity of green powder. Burned papers were found in the stove.

According to Henry's declarations, he had left in his lodging three and a half kilos of picric acid, which were to serve him in making twelve or fifteen other bombs if, as he had counted on, he had escaped justice after the first explosion.

It is thus obvious that the authors of the break-in intended to remove the rest of the explosive substances he'd prepared.

La Rue des Bons-Enfants

The offices of the Compagnie des Mines de Carmaux occu-pied the mezzanine of a house at 11 Avenue de l'Opéra. A second exit opens onto the Rue d'Argenteuil. On November 8, 1892, between 11:00 and 11:30 a.m., M. Berlich, wanting to speak to the chief accountant, M. Bellois, climbed the stairs without meeting anyone. In the left-hand corner of the landing he noticed a voluminous object leaning against the door, which he had to step over in order to enter.

A few instants later M. Bellois, who accompanied him out, noticed the same package, remarked that it was quite heavy, and called M. Auguenard, the cashier, as well as the office boy Garin. They tore the newspaper that was wrapped around it, attached by a string, and they saw a cast iron kettle whose flipped-over cover was held in place by a band or strip of sheet metal attached to the two handles. It was resting on the cover, its bottom in the air. The concierge Garnier and the office boy carefully took it downstairs to the Rue d'Argenteuil and placed it on the sidewalk. A large group gathered around the device and several people noticed a white powder whose tiny grains had escaped from the gaps in the cover.

The office boy called over Police Officer Cartier, who was charged with crossing the children coming out of the school on the Rue d'Argenteuil. Cartier, held back by his assignment, was unable to carry the kettle, but at this moment Sub-Brigadier Fomorin and Agent Réaux arrived, whom he informed of the events. The concierge gave them a briefcase, the device was placed in it, and Garin, accompanied by Fomorin and Réaux, carried it to the commissariat of the Palais-Royal quarter.

The house where the commissariat is located is on the Rue des Bons-Enfants. It is made up of a central building and two wings framing a courtyard that opens onto the street by a porte cochère. The offices were on the second floor of the left wing.

It was exactly 11:35 a.m. when the sub-brigadier, the policeman, and Garin entered the courtyard. As they were crossing it Garin said to Réaux, "It's heavy, it wouldn't hurt if you gave me some help." The policeman went to his assistance and all three of them started climbing the staircase. Barely two minutes had passed when a tremendous explosion resounded.

When people entered the commissariat they found themselves before an unspeakable horror. In the vestibule a corpse was lying in the middle of the debris, face down. His clothing had almost completely disappeared and the flesh had taken on a grayish hue. It was the policeman Réaux, his two legs torn off below the knees, his thighs crushed, his face and hands carbonized.

In the waiting room, which was next to the vestibule, the destruction was total. It was there that the device had exploded. The floorboards were collapsed. There was a pile of shattered debris, torn-up pieces of wood, clothing, and shreds of flesh. A packet of guts hung from a gas jet in the ceiling.

The walls were spattered with blood. Near the window, people literally walked on shreds of flesh, liver, and lungs. The explosion had caused four victims in this room: Sub-Brigadier Fomorin; the office boy Garin; the secretary of the commissariat Pousset, whose body had barely preserved a human form; and Inspector Troutot who, despite his horrible wounds, was still in his death throes. He died during the day.

The first elements of the investigation were provided by the newspaper that the device was wrapped in. It was the June 1, 1892, issue of *Le Temps*. It was supposed that the assassin hadn't saved it without reason, but rather because it contained some information of special interest to him. This issue related the arrest of the Henry brothers, an arrest that had taken place on May 30 but that hadn't been sustained. The investigation soon established that of these two anarchists, one, Fortuné, was in Bourges on November 8. Suspicion thus fell on Émile Henry.

In July, he had been pointed out as engaging in suspicious studies of chemistry. On November 8, he left the shop of his boss, M. Dupuis, around 10:15 a.m. and didn't return until noon. According to Mme Dupuis he had demonstrated violent emotions when his boss returned with a newspaper with an account of the catastrophe. The next day he said he wasn't feeling well and on November 10 at four he left his office under the pretext of going to his mother to be taken care of. Instead of going to Brévannes he went to London, where two or three days later he charged a friend with mailing from Orléans a letter to M. Dupuis. In that letter he declared that though stranger to the crime on the Rue des Bons-Enfants "He really didn't care to spend months in preventive detention before the arrest of the real authors of the explosion."

Despite all these suspicious circumstances there were no positive charges against him. And even the first verification of how he spent his time the morning of November 8 seemed favorable to him. Having left the Rue de Rocroi around ten he had returned by noon, having done the shopping he'd been charged with on the Rue Tronchet and the Boulevard de Courcelles. The distances are considerable and, unless he was extraordinarily fast, he wouldn't have had the time during the interval of two hours to carry the bomb to the Avenue de l'Opéra.

Arrested after the crime at the Café Terminus, he invoked that alibi and persisted in his denials until February 23. But on that day, placed in the presence of other anarchists suspected of having participated in the attack of November 8, he renounced this system and declared that he alone was guilty. He then gave detailed explanations of the conception and execution of the crime.

He had resolved to prove to the miners of Carmaux, exploited by ambitious men, that only the anarchists were capable of dedication. One evening, he went to 11 Avenue de l'Opera and verified through the plaque on the wall that the mining company had its offices there. The door was closed and he wasn't able to enter the building to study its layout. Shortly afterward he returned in the middle of the day and climbed to the upper floors. Thus informed, he constructed the device.

He possessed twenty dynamite cartridges whose provenance he refuses to divulge and resolved to fabricate a bomb. In order to make the detonator he procured a metal case for 1.50 francs from the stationary shop of Madame Colin, 107 Rue Lafayette. On November 4 at 7:00 p.m. he purchased four kilograms of potassium chlorate at 4 francs the kilogram at the Billaut chemical store, Place de la Sorbonne. He received a 10 percent discount saying he was an assistant in a school in Saint-Denis and only paid 14.40 francs. He also requested one hundred grams of sodium, but this product not being able to be handled in the light he was asked to come back the next day. On November 5 at noon, he came back to get the flask and paid 2.65 francs.

He fabricated the detonator according to a known system. The reversing of the device placed water in contact with sodium, which, having caught fire, would in turn detonate three primers of fulminate of mercury. This done he purchased a kettle at M. Comte's hardware store on the Rue Lepic for 3.30 francs. In the middle he placed the detonator, which he surrounded with twenty dynamite cartridges, then filled the empty space with four kilograms of chlorate of potassium, mixed with an equal quantity of powdered sugar. He secured the cover with a band, being careful to turn it over.

On November 8, he left his office a little after ten and took a car to go to the Rue Tronchet, where he arrived at about ten fifteen. He carried out his commission in an instant, took a second car, and had himself taken to the Place Blanche. It was then about ten thirty. He then rapidly went on foot to the Rue Véron, took the bomb from a closet, returned to the Place Blanche, took a third car, and had himself taken to the Avenue de l'Opéra. He got out some distance from number eleven, but since he was still overheated from running around, he stopped in front of a store after having placed the bomb on the sidewalk.

After a short time, thinking that he had been noticed by a concierge and in a hurry to be done, he picked it up and entered the vestibule of number eleven. He passed two people who didn't notice him, climbed the staircase, and came back down almost immediately, after having placed the device at the door of the office, the cover on the bottom. Once he left the house he took a fourth car, went to the Boulevard de Courcelles, where he arrived at around eleven thirty, and, his commissions done, he returned on foot to the Rue Rocroi.

He had foreseen the possibility that the device would be taken away by the police: "According to my experience," he said at his interrogation of February 24, "I supposed that the kettle would explode five or six minutes after having been placed in front of the door of the offices of the Carmaux Company, but I wasn't unaware that if the kettle was taken away before the explosion it would be carried to the neighborhood police commissariat, so that if the rich people on the Avenue de l'Opéra were to escape the fate I had in store for them I was certain of hitting the police, who were also my enemy."

It is certain that Henry knew the layout of the house. He described it exactly and, taken to the site, he went without hesitation to the spot where the bomb was found.

The precise description he gave of the device is in absolute agreement with the statements of the experts, Messieurs Vielle and Girard.

He wasn't recognized by the personnel of the Comte hardware store, but all the indications he gave concerning the store, the kettle he purchased, and the prices are in conformity with reality. The same holds true for the metal case. As for his acquisitions on the Place de la Sorbonne it is proven that on the date and at the time he indicated the Billaut store received a payment of 14.40 francs. Finally, it is demonstrated that the itinerary followed by Henry on November 8 can be easily carried out under the conditions he specified.

The proof of his guilt is thus clearly established. It emerges from the evidence in all the statements that at all points corroborate the accused's declarations.

From Jean Maitron, *Ravachol et les Anarchistes*, Paris: Julliard, 1964

The Courtroom Interrogation of Émile Henry

Q: On February 12 you entered the Café Terminus.
A: Yes, at eight o'clock.

Q: Your bomb was in your pants belt.
A: No, in my overcoat pocket.

Q: Why did you go to the Café Terminus?
A: I had first gone to Bignon, the Café de la Paix, and the Américain but there weren't enough people. So I went to the Terminus and I waited.

Q: There was an orchestra. How long did you wait?
A: An hour.

Q: Why?
A: So that there would be a bigger crowd.

Q: And then?
A: You know full well.

Q: I'm asking you.
A: I threw away my cigar! I lit the fuse and then taking the bomb in my hand I left and, as I was leaving the café, from the doorway I threw the bomb.

Q: You hold human life in contempt.
A: No, the life of bourgeois.

Q: You did everything you could to save yours.

A: Yes, so I could start again. I counted on leaving the café, closing the door, getting a ticket at the Saint-Lazare station, escaping, and starting over the next day.

Q: As you left you met a waiter. Further on a certain Etienne detained you saying: "I've got you, you wretch!" You answered: "Not yet." What did you then do?
A: I fired at him.

Q: He fell. What did you say?
A: That he was lucky that I didn't have a better revolver.

Q: Then you were detained by a hairdresser. What did you do?
A: I shot him with the revolver.

Q: He was hit and hasn't healed. Agent Poisson followed you.
A: At this moment, since a crowd was gathering, I stopped. I waited for Agent Poisson and fired three shots at him with my revolver.

Q: You were then arrested, and the policemen had a hard time wresting you from the fury of the crowd.
A: Which didn't know what I'd done.

Q: You had special bullets on you. Why?
A: To cause more harm.

Q: And a dagger on which there was a preparation.
A: I had poisoned the blade in order to strike an anarchist informer.

Q: You were determined to strike the agent with that weapon?

A: Certainly.

Q: You were seated at a table near the door and had thrown the device in front of you. Why didn't you hit more people with that explosion, since you had aimed at the orchestra?

A: I threw the bomb too high. It hit a lamp and went off course.

Q: A muffled explosion was heard and the café was completely destroyed; tables, mirrors, woodwork were broken. There were many wounded, twenty. One of them, M. Borde, has since died. His leg was covered with wounds. Another, M. Van Herreweghen, received forty wounds. There were women: Mme Kingsbourg, who is still suffering from her wounds, and many others that you will hear. And these women were so terrified that they have hidden their presence and their wounds. You said that the more bourgeois that die the better it would be.

A: That's just what I think.

Q: At first you said you were called Breton. A little later you revealed yourself and you said that your name is Émile Henry and you gave the design of your device. How was it made?

A: It was a small kettle of tin containing a detonator and a fuse.

Q: You said that you had been relatively unsuccessful. What does that mean?

A: I wanted to kill more, but the kettle wasn't properly closed.

Q: You had put projectiles in it.
A: I had put 120 pellets.

Q: Vaillant, who said he wanted to wound and not kill, had put nails and not pellets.
A: Me, I wanted to kill and not wound.

Q: Your domicile wasn't known.
A: I had said that I didn't have a domicile in Paris. I declared that I arrived from Marseilles or Peking.

Q: Soon afterward a room at the Villa Faucheur was robbed. The police superintendent found explosives and recognized that this was your home.
A: I don't know who robbed my home.

Q: You were warned that your domicile has been discovered and at that point you declared that quantities of explosives must have been found at your home.
A: I had enough to make twelve to fifteen bombs.

Q: (To the jury) You know the crime and the accused, who has just cynically confessed his crime.
A: It's not cynicism, it's conviction.

Q: Did you want to kill the waiter Etienne?
A: I wanted to kill all those who put themselves in the way of my escape.

Q: Did you want to kill the agent Poisson?
A: Certainly. His saber was raised and he would have killed me.

Q: Did you want to kill the people at the Hôtel Terminus?
A: Certainly, as many as possible.

Q: Did you want to destroy the building?
A: Oh, I could care less!

The presiding judge to the jury: This would suffice to establish the guilt of the accused. But whatever the crime, justice—and this is our honor—never deviates from the usual rules. We must examine all the details and pause before another act for which the accused is reproached.

Q: Your father lived at Brévannes, then he went to Spain, after taking part in the Paris Commune, and your mother found herself a widow with three children. You received a grant at the École J-B Say, at seventeen you qualified for admission to the École Polytechnique. You didn't continue.
A: In order not to be a soldier and be forced to fire on the unfortunate, like at Fourmies.

Q: You found a job with a builder, M. Bordenave, your relative. How much did you earn?
A: In Venice I earned 100 F a month.

Q: Why did you leave?
A: For reasons foreign to this affair.

Q: You said that he wanted to force you to carry out a secret surveillance, which revolted you. When he was questioned M. Bordenave protested.
A: He recognized that there was a misunderstanding.

Q: You then found another job.
A: I suffered through three months of poverty before that!

Q: In any event, you soon had a position.
A: A quite mediocre one: 100 to 120 F a month.

Q: At this moment you come under the influence of one of your brothers. A short while later you were arrested after a meeting in honor of Ravachol, and your boss found anarchist works in your desk, most notably a translation of an Italian newspaper indicating how to make nitroglycerine and in which we read: "Long live theft, long live dynamite!" We can see there the rules you put in practice in the attack on the Rue des Bons-Enfants. So then your boss fired you.
A: I was fired when these papers were found.

Q: You looked for work at a watchmaker's. Then you were employed by *L'Endehors*, edited by Matha, who was condemned in 1892—the year you arrived at the newspaper—for inciting insubordination among soldiers. You refused to be a soldier.
A: I had done three years of school battalion and that was all I could do as a soldier.

Q: You avoided the call to military service and your mother disapproved of you.
A: She feared my expatriation.

Q: On the recommendation of Ortiz, a burglar, you went to work for M. Dupuis.

A: I don't know what Ortiz has done since I knew him.

Q: M. Dupuis had increased your salary.

A: I had much affection for him.

Q: Would you like to repeat before the jury the confessions you made during the questioning? I would very much like it to be you that speaks.

A: Certainly. Tomorrow I'll give the motives for my act. The Société des Carmaux is represented in Paris by its administration. After the strike I bought a kettle. I had dynamite, a primer, and fuses.

The questioning continues. The accused refuses to say what he did during 1893. During a difficult period in the questioning, the presiding judge shouts:

Q: Beware of your silence!

A: I don't care. I don't have to beware of my silence. I know full well that I'll be condemned to death.

Q: Listen; I think there's a confession that's damaging to your pride. Vaillant admitted that he received 100 F from a burglar. You don't want to recognize that you extended your hand to receive the money from a theft, the hand that we today see covered in blood.

A: My hands are covered in blood, like your red robe is! In any case, I don't have to answer you.

Q: You are accused and it's my duty to interrogate you.

A: I don't recognize your justice.

Q: You don't recognize justice. Unfortunately for you, you are in its hands, and the jury will be able to appreciate this.
A: I know!

(The presiding judge): Be seated.

From Jean Maitron, *Ravachol et les Anarchistes*, Paris: Julliard, 1964.

Émile Henry's Defense Speech

It is not a defense that I present to you. I am not in any way seeking to escape the reprisals of the society I have attacked. Besides, I acknowledge only one tribunal—myself—and the verdict of any other is meaningless to me. I wish merely to give you an explanation of my acts and to tell you how I was led to perform them.

I have been an anarchist for only a short time. It was as recently as the middle of 1891 that I entered the revolutionary movement. Up to that time, I had lived in circles entirely imbued with current morality. I had been accustomed to respect and even to love the principles of fatherland and family, of authority and property.

For teachers in the present generation too often forget one thing: it is that life, with its struggles and defeats, its injustices and iniquities, takes upon itself indiscreetly to open the eyes of the ignorant to reality. This happened to me, as it happens to everyone. I had been told that life was easy, that it was wide open to those who were intelligent and energetic; experience showed me that only the cynical and the servile were able to secure good seats at the banquet.

I had been told that our social institutions were founded on justice and equality; I observed all around me nothing but lies and impostures.

Each day I shed an illusion. Everywhere I went, I witnessed the same miseries among some, and the same joys among others. I was not slow to understand that the grand words I had been taught to venerate: honor, devotion, duty, were only the mask that concealed the most shameful baseness.

The manufacturer who created a colossal fortune out of the toil of workers who lacked everything was an honest gentleman. The deputy and the minister, their hands ever open for bribes, were devoted to the public good. The officer who experimented with a new type of rifle on children of seven had done his duty, and, openly in parliament, the president of the council congratulated him! Everything I saw revolted me, and my intelligence was attracted by criticism of the existing social organization. Such criticism has been made too often for me to repeat it. It is enough to say that I became the enemy of a society that I judged to be criminal.

Drawn at first to socialism, I was not slow in separating myself from that party. I have too much love of freedom, too much respect for individual initiative, too much repugnance for military organization to assume a number in the ordered army of the fourth estate. Besides, I realized that basically socialism changes nothing in the existing order. It maintains the principle of authority, and, whatever self-styled free-thinkers may say about it, that principle is no more than the antiquated survival of faith in a superior power.

Scientific studies gradually made me aware of the play of natural forces in the universe. I became materialist and atheist; I came to realize that modern science discards the hypothesis of God, of which it has no need. In the same way, religious and authoritarian morality, which are based on false assumptions, should be allowed to disappear. What then, I asked myself, was the new morality in harmony with the laws of nature that might regenerate the old world and give birth to a happy humanity?

It was at this moment that I came into contact with a group of anarchist comrades whom I consider, even today, among the best I have ever known. The character of these men immediately captivated me. I discerned in them a great sincerity, a total frankness, a searching distrust of all prejudices, and I wanted to understand the idea that produced men so different from anyone I had encountered up to that point.

The idea—as soon as I embraced it—found in my mind a soil completely prepared by observation and personal reflection to receive it. It merely gave precision to what already existed there in vague and wavering form. In my turn I became an anarchist.

I do not need to develop on this occasion the whole theory of anarchism. I merely wish to emphasize its revolutionary aspect, the destructive and negative aspect that brings me here before you.

At this moment of embittered struggle between the middle class and its enemies, I am almost tempted to say, with Souvarine in *Germinal*: "All discussions about the future are criminal, since they hinder pure and simple destruction and slow down the march of the revolution."

I brought with me into the struggle a profound hatred, which every day was renewed by the spectacle of this society where everything is base, everything is equivocal, everything is ugly, where everything is an impediment to the outflow of human passions, to the generous impulses of the heart, to the free flight of thought.

I wanted to strike as strongly and as justly as I could. Let us start then with the first attempt I made, the explosion in the Rue des Bon-Enfants. I had followed closely the events at Carmaux. The first news of the strike had filled me with joy. The miners seemed at last to have abandoned those useless pacific strikes in which the trusting worker patiently waits for his few francs to triumph over the company's millions. They seemed to have entered on a way of violence that manifested itself resolutely on August 15, 1892. The offices and buildings of the mine were invaded by a crowd of people tired of suffering without reprisals; justice was about to be wrought on the engineer whom his workers so deeply hated, when the timorous ones chose to interfere.

Who were these men? The same who cause the miscarriage of all revolutionary movements because they fear that the people, once they act freely, will no longer obey their voices; those who persuade thousands of men to endure privations month after month so as to beat the drum over their sufferings and create for themselves a popularity that will put them into office: such men—I mean the socialist leaders—in fact assumed the leadership of the strike movement.

Immediately a wave of glib gentlemen appeared in the region; they put themselves entirely at the disposition of the struggle, organized subscriptions, arranged conferences, and appealed on all sides for funds. The miners surrendered all initiative into their hands, and what happened, everyone knows.

The strike went on and on, and the miners established the most intimate acquaintance with hunger, which became their habitual companion; they used up the tiny reserve fund of their syndicate and of the other organizations that came to their help, and then, at the end of two months, they returned crestfallen to their pit, more wretched than ever before. It would have been so simple in the beginning to have attacked the Company in its only sensitive spot, the financial one; to have burnt the stocks of coal, to have broken the mining machines, to have demolished the drainage pumps.

Then, certainly, the Company would have very soon capitulated. But the great pontiffs of socialism would not allow such procedures because they are anarchist procedures. At such games one runs the risk of prison and—who knows?—perhaps one of those bullets that performed so miraculously at Fourmies? That is not the way to win seats on municipal councils or in legislatures. In brief, having been momentarily troubled, order reigned once again at Carmaux.

More powerful than ever, the Company continued its exploitation, and the gentlemen shareholders congratulated themselves on the happy outcome of the strike. Their dividends would be even more pleasant to gather in.

It was then that I decided to intrude among that concert of happy tones a voice the bourgeois had already heard but which they thought had died with Ravachol: the voice of dynamite.

I wanted to show the bourgeoisie that henceforward their pleasures would not be untouched, that their insolent triumphs would be disturbed, that their golden calf would rock violently on its pedestal until the final shock that would cast it down among filth and blood.

At the same time I wanted to make the miners understand that there is only one category of men, the anarchists, who sincerely resent their sufferings and are willing to avenge them. Such men do not sit in parliament like Monsieur Guesde and his associates, but they march to the guillotine.

So I prepared a bomb. At one stage the accusation that had been thrown at Ravachol came to my memory. What about the innocent victims? I soon resolved that question. The building where the Carmaux Company had its offices was inhabited only by bourgeois; hence there would be no innocent victims. The whole of the bourgeoisie lives by the exploitation of the unfortunate, and should expiate its crimes together. So it was with absolute confidence in the legitimacy of my deed that I left my bomb before the door to the Company's offices.

I have already explained my hope, in case my device was discovered before it exploded, that it would go off in the police station, where those it harmed would still be my enemies. Such were the motives that led me to commit the first attempt of which I have been accused.

Let us go on to the second incident, of the Café Terminus. I had returned to Paris at the time of the Vaillant affair, and I witnessed the frightful repression that followed the explosion at the Palais Bourbon. I saw the draconian measures that the government decided to take against the anarchists. Everywhere there were spies, and searches, and arrests. A crowd of individuals were indiscriminately rounded up, torn from their families, and thrown into prison. Nobody was concerned about what happened to the wives and children of these comrades while they remained in jail.

The anarchist was no longer regarded as a man, but as a wild beast to be hunted everywhere while the bourgeois press, which is the vile slave of authority, loudly demands his extermination.

At the same time, anarchist papers and pamphlets were seized and the right of meeting was abrogated. Worse than that: when it seemed desirable to get one comrade completely out of the way, an informer came and left in his room a packet that he said contained tannin; the next day a search was made, on a warrant dated the previous day, a box of suspicious powders was found, the comrade was taken to court and sentenced to three years in jail. If you wish to know the truth of that, ask the wretched spy who found his way into the home of comrade Mérigeaud!

But all such procedures were good because they struck at an enemy who had spread fear, and those who had trembled wanted to display their courage. As the crown of that crusade against the heretics, we heard M. Reynal, Minister of the Interior, declare in the Chamber of Deputies that the measures taken by the government had thrown terror into the camp of the anarchists. But that was not yet enough. A man who had killed nobody was condemned to death. It was necessary to appear brave right to the end, and one fine morning he was guillotined.

But, gentlemen of the bourgeoisie, you have reckoned a little too much without your host. You arrested hundreds of men and women, you violated scores of homes, but still outside the prison walls there were men unknown to you who watched from the shadows as you hunted the anarchists, and waited only for the moment that would be favorable for them in their turn to hunt the hunters.

Reynal's words were a challenge thrown before the anarchists. The gauntlet was taken up. The bomb in the Café Terminus is the answer to all your violations of freedom, to your arrests, to your searches, to your laws against the press, to your mass transportations, to your guillotinings. But why, you ask, attack these peaceful café guests, who sat listening to music and who, no doubt, were neither judges nor deputies nor bureaucrats? Why? It is very simple. The bourgeoisie did not distinguish among the anarchists. Vaillant, a man on his own, threw a bomb; nine tenths of the comrades did not even know him. But that meant nothing; the persecution was a mass one, and anyone with the slightest anarchist links was hunted down. And since you hold a whole party responsible for the actions of a single man, and strike indiscriminately, we also strike indiscriminately.

Perhaps we should attack only the deputies who make laws against us, the judges who apply those laws, the police who arrest us? I do not agree. These men are only instruments. They do not act in their own name. Their functions were instituted by the bourgeoisie for its own defense. They are no more guilty than the rest of you. Those good bourgeois who hold no office but who reap their dividends and live idly on the profits of the workers' toil, they also must take their share in the reprisals. And not only they, but all those who are satisfied with the existing order, who applaud the acts of the government and so become its accomplices, those clerks earning three or five hundred francs a month who hate the people even more violently than the rich, that stupid and pretentious mass of folk who always choose the strongest side—in other words, the daily clientele of Terminus and the other great cafés.

That is why I struck at random and did not choose my victims! The bourgeoisie must be brought to understand that those who have suffered have finally grown tired of their sufferings; they are showing their teeth and they will strike all the more brutally if you are brutal with them. They have no respect for human life, because the bourgeoisie themselves have shown they have no care for it. It is not for the assassins who were responsible for the bloody week and for Fourmies to regard others as assassins.

We will not spare the women and children of the bourgeois, for the women and children of those we love have not been spared. Must we not count among the innocent victims those children who die slowly of anemia in the slums because bread is scarce in their houses; those women who grow pale in your workshops, working to earn forty sous a day and fortunate when poverty does not force them into prostitution; those old men whom you have made production machines all their lives and whom you cast onto the waste heap or into the workhouse when their strength has worn away?

At least have the courage of your crimes, gentlemen of the bourgeoisie, and grant that our reprisals are completely legitimate.

Of course, I am under no illusions. I know my deeds will not yet be understood by the masses who are unprepared for them. Even among the workers, for whom I have fought, there will be many, misled by your newspapers, who will regard me as their enemy. But that does not matter. I am not concerned with anyone's judgment. Nor am I ignorant of the fact that there are individuals claiming to be anarchists who hasten to disclaim any solidarity with the propagandists of the deed. They seek to establish a subtle distinction between the theoreticians and the terrorists. Too cowardly to risk their own lives, they deny those who act. But the influence they pretend to wield over the revolutionary movement is nil. Today the field is open to action, without weakness or retreat.

Alexander Herzen, the Russian revolutionary, once said: "Of two things one must be chosen: to condemn and march forward, or to pardon and turn back halfway." We intend neither to pardon nor to turn back, and we shall always march forward until the revolution, which is the goal of our efforts, finally arrives to crown our work with the creation of a free world.

In that pitiless war that we have declared on the bourgeoisie, we ask for no pity. We give death, and we know how to endure it. So it is with indifference that I await your verdict. I know that my head is not the last you will cut off; yet others will fall, for the starving are beginning to know the way to your great cafés and restaurants, to the Terminus and Foyot. You will add other names to the bloody list of our dead.

You have hanged in Chicago, decapitated in Germany, garroted in Jerez, shot in Barcelona, guillotined in Montbrison and Paris, but what you will never destroy is anarchy. Its roots are too deep. It is born in the heart of a society that is rotting and falling apart. It is a violent reaction against the established order. It represents all the egalitarian and libertarian aspirations that strike out against authority. It is everywhere, which makes it impossible to contain. It will end by killing you.

From "Anarchist Encyclopedia" in *Gazette des Tribunaux*, April 27–28, 1894. Translated by George Woodcock and revised by Mitchell Abidor.

Letter to the Director of the Conciergerie

During the visit you made to my cell Sunday, the 18th of this month, we had a quite friendly discussion of anarchist ideas.

You said you were very surprised to learn our theories in a different light, and you asked me to summarize our conversation in writing, so you could better know what the anarchists want.

You can easily understand, monsieur, that in just a few pages one can't expound upon a theory that analyses our current social life in all of its manifestations; that studies these manifestations the way a doctor examines a sick body; and that then condemns them because they're contrary to human happiness and, in place of them, builds an entirely new life, based on principles completely antagonistic to those upon which the old society was built.

Besides, others have already done what you ask of me: Kropotkin, Reclus, Sébastien Faure have set forth their ideas, and pushed their development as far as possible.

Read *Évolution et Révolution* by Reclus; *La Morale Anarchiste*, *Les Paroles d'un Révolté*, *La Conquête du Pain* by Peter Kropotkin; *Autorité et Liberté*, *Le Machinisme et ses Conséquences* by Sébastien Faure; *La Société Mourante et l'Anarchie* by Grave; *Entre Paysans* (Fra Contadini) by Malatesta; read also the numerous pamphlets and manifestoes that have appeared over the last fifteen years, each expounding new ideas, according to whether study or circumstances suggested them to their authors.

Read all of this and then you will form a well-founded judgment on anarchy.

Nevertheless, don't think that anarchism is a dogma, a doctrine that can't be attacked, indisputable, venerated by its followers as the Koran is by Muslims.

No, the absolute freedom that we call for ceaselessly expands our ideas, raises them toward new horizons (following the will of diverse individuals), and removes them from the rigid frameworks of regimentation and codification.

We are not "believers"; we don't bow before Reclus or Kropotkin. We debate their ideas, we accept them when they develop sympathetic impressions in our brains, but we reject them when they don't strike a chord within us.

We are far from possessing the blind faith of the collectivists, who believe in something because Guesde said it had to be believed in, and who have a catechism whose paragraphs it would be sacrilegious to dispute.

This being established, I am going to try to briefly and rapidly expound for you what *I* understand by anarchy, without involving other comrades who on certain points could have views different from mine.

You would not dispute the fact that the current social system is evil, and the proof that it is, is that everyone suffers from it. From the poor itinerant, with neither bread nor roof, who knows constant hunger, to the millionaire, who lives in fear of a revolt of the poor that would trouble his digestion, all of humanity lives in a state of anxiety.

On what foundations does bourgeois society rest? Putting aside the principles of family, fatherland, and religion, which are nothing but corollaries, we can affirm that that the two cornerstones, the two fundamental principles of the current state are authority and property.

I don't want to go on any longer on this subject: it would be easy for me to prove that all the ills we suffer from flow from property and authority.

Poverty, theft, crime, prostitution, war, revolution are all nothing but the results of these principles.

The two foundations of society being thus evil, there is no reason to hesitate. There's no need to try any of a group of palliatives (e.g., socialism) that serve only to shift the wrong. The two vicious germs must be destroyed, and eradicated from social life.

This is why we anarchists want to replace private property with communism, and authority with freedom.

No more deeds of ownership or domination: absolute equality.

When we say absolute equality we don't claim that all men will have the same brain, the same physical organization: we know that there will always be the greatest diversity in cerebral and physical aptitudes. It is precisely this variety of capacities that will bring into being the production of all that is necessary for humanity, and we count on this as well to maintain emulation in an anarchist society.

There will be engineers and laborers: this is obvious. But one will not be considered superior to the other, since the work of the engineer is useless without the collaboration of the laborer, and vice versa.

Everyone being free to choose his trade there will only exist beings who obey, without any constraints, the leanings nature places in them (the guarantee of good productivity).

Here a question must be asked: And the lazy? Will everyone want to work?

We answer yes, everyone will want to work, and here is why:

Today, the average workday is ten hours.

Many workers are kept busy at labors that are absolutely useless to society, in particular on armaments for the army and navy. Many are also unemployed. Add to this a considerable number of able-bodied men who produce nothing: soldiers, priests, policemen, magistrates, civil servants, etc.

We can thus say, without being accused of exaggeration, that of a hundred capable of producing some kind of labor, only fifty furnish an effort truly useful to society. It is these fifty who produce all of society's riches.

From this flows the deduction that if everyone worked, instead of ten hours the workday would decrease to only five.

Beyond this we should consider that in the current state of things the total of manufactured products is four times, and of agricultural products three times, the amount required to meet humanity's needs; which is to say that a humanity three times more numerous would be clothed, housed, heated, and fed; in a word, would have all of its needs satisfied if waste and other causes didn't destroy that overproduction. (You will find these statistics in the little pamphlet: *The Products of the Land and of Industry*.)

From what has gone before, we can draw the following conclusion:

A society where all would work together, and which would be satisfied with productivity not far beyond its consumer needs (the excess of the first over the second would constitute a small reserve) would have to ask of each of its able-bodied members an effort of only two or three hours, perhaps less.

Who would then refuse to give such a small quantity of labor? Who would want to live with the shame of being held in contempt by all and being considered a parasite?

. . . Property and authority march together, the one supporting the other to keep humanity enslaved.

What is the right to property? Is it a natural right? Is it legitimate that one eats while the other fasts? No. Nature, in creating us, made us with similar organisms, and the laborer's stomach demands the same satisfaction as that of the financier.

Nevertheless, one class today has taken all, stealing from the other class the bread not only of its body, but also of its soul.

Yes, in a century that we call one of progress and science, is it not painful to think of the millions of intelligences hungry for knowledge and that cannot flourish? How many children of the common man, who could have become men and women of great value, useful to humanity, will never know anything but the few indispensable notions taught in elementary school?

Property! That is the enemy of human happiness, for it alone creates inequality, and in its train hatred, envy, bloody revolt . . .

Established authority serves no other purpose than the sanctioning of property. It is there to put force at the service of the act of despoiling.

Work being a natural need, you will accept along with me that no one would flee from the demand of as minimal an effort as that which we spoke of above.

(Labor is so natural a need that hstory shows us several statesmen treating themselves with joy from the cares of politics to work as simple laborers: To cite two well-known cases: Louis XVI worked with locks, and in our day Gladstone, "The Great Old Man" [in English in the original −ed.] profits from his vacations to himself chop down some of the oaks of his forests, like a common lumberjack.)

So you see, monsieur, there would be no reason to resort to the law to avoid the problem of idlers.

But if in some extraordinary case someone wanted to refuse his assistance to his brothers, it would *still* be less costly to feed this unfortunate, who can only be described as sick, than to maintain legislators, magistrates, police, and prison wardens to break him down.

Many other questions arise, but they are of a secondary nature; the most important thing being to establish that the suppression of property would not cause a cessation of production due to the development of laziness, and that anarchist society would know how to feed itself and satisfy all of its needs.

All the other objections that can be raised will be easily refuted by taking inspiration from the idea that an anarchist milieu would cause the love of and solidarity with his fellows to grow in each of its members, for man will know that in working for others he works for himself.

A seemingly better-founded objection is the following:

If there is no more authority, if there is no fear of the gendarme to stop the criminal's arm, don't we risk seeing crimes and misdemeanors multiply at a frightening rate?

The answer is simple:

We can categorize the crimes committed today in two principal categories: crimes of interest and crimes of passion.

The first group will disappear on its own, since there can be no attacks on property in an environment that has done away with property.

As for the second group, no law can stop them. Far from this being the case, the current law—which acquits a husband who kills his adulterous wife—does nothing but favor the frequency of these crimes.

On the contrary, an anarchist environment would raise the moral level of humanity. Man will understand that he has no rights over a woman who gives herself to another man, since that woman does nothing but follow her nature.

Consequently crimes, in a future society, will become increasingly rare, until they disappear completely.

Monsieur, I am going to summarize for you my ideal of an anarchist society.

No more authority, which is far more contrary to human happiness than the few excesses that could occur at the beginning of a free society.

In place of the current authoritarian organization, the grouping of individuals by sympathies and affinities without laws or leaders.

No more private property; the gathering in common of products; each one working and consuming according to his needs, which is to say, as he wishes.

No more family, selfish and bourgeois, making man the property of woman and woman the property of man; no more demanding of two beings who loved each other for but a moment that they remain attached till the end of their days.

Nature is capricious: it always demands new sensations. It wants free love. This is why we want free unions.

No more fatherlands, no more hatred between brothers, pitting against each other men who have never set eyes on each other.

Replacement of the narrow and petty attachment of the chauvinist for his country by the large and fruitful love of all of humanity, without distinction of race or color.

No more religions, forged by priests to degrade the masses and give them the hope of a better life, while they themselves enjoy life in the here and now.

On the contrary, the continual expansion of the sciences, put within the grasp of every being who will feel attached to their study, little by little bringing all men to a materialist consciousness.

The particular study of hypnotic phenomena, which science is beginning to become aware of, in order to unmask the charlatans who present to the ignorant, in a marvelous and superstitious light, facts that are purely physical.

In a word, absolutely no more hindrances to the free development of human nature.

The free blossoming of physical, cerebral, and mental faculties.

I am not so optimistic as to believe that a society built on such foundations will arrive at perfect harmony. But I have the profound conviction that two or three generations will suffice to tear mankind from the influence of the artificial civilization that it submits to today and to return it to the state of nature, which is the state of goodness and of love.

But in order to make this ideal victorious, to set anarchist society on a solid foundation, we must begin with the work of destruction. The old, worm-eaten edifice must be torn down.

This is what we are doing.

The bourgeoisie claims that we will never arrive at our goal.

The future, the very near future, will teach them.

Jean Maitron, *Ravachol et les Anarchistes*. This text was written from jail just two weeks after Henry had thrown a bomb at Paris's Café Terminus, killing one and injuring twenty.

■ FOR ÉMILE HENRY

Émile Henry
By Victor Serge

I think that acts of brutal revolt strike their target, for they awaken the masses, shake them up with the lashing of a whip, and show the real face of the bourgeoisie, still trembling at the moment the rebel climbs the gallows.

To those who say to you that hatred doesn't engender love, answer that it is living love that often engenders hatred.

First, a few words to the comrades.

Let them not reproach me for glorifying a man, making him into a banner. We want neither tribunes nor martyrs nor prophets. But in order to be strong you have to know yourself, and in order to better support the struggles of today you have to know the joys and fears of past hours. And then it is so good, in this world governed by so many crooked interests, among the base masks that surround us, to once again see the clear profiles of those who were able to be honest in a humanity of brutes.

I will also not write an apology for murder of whatever kind. Murders will be the most painful page in our history. And it is certainly one of society's greatest crimes to have forced us, we who want peace and love, to shed blood.

On May 21, 1894, Émile Henry, twenty-one and a half years old, died on the gallows at La Roquette Prison in Paris.

The previous April 28, he had been sentenced to death by the jury of the Seine, having admitted his guilt in a series of terrorist attacks: "The explosion on the Rue des Bons-Enfants that killed five people and led to the death of a sixth; the explosion at the Café Terminus that killed one person, mortally wounded another, and wounded a number of others; finally, six shots fired at those who pursued him." He had acted with complete lucidity and never once sought to attenuate the terror his acts inspired.

He was twenty-one; it was the springtime of his life; it was the month of May, the spring of nature; and though the death sentence was certain, his tranquil courage, made up of intelligence and enthusiasm, never flagged for a second.

He was the son of a worker and a worker himself, having worked in a shop. A rational education backed by a remarkable spirit of logic and observation led him to anarchism. At first, simply revolted by the sight of social injustice he became a socialist. "Attracted to socialism for a moment," he said, "it didn't take long for me to move away from the party. I loved freedom too much, had too much respect for individual initiative, too much repugnance for being part of a group to take a number in the matriculated army of the Fourth Estate. In any case, I saw that in the end socialism changes nothing of the current order. It maintains the authoritarian principle and this principle, whatever so-called free-thinkers might say, is nothing but a holdover of faith in a supreme power." His studies showed anarchism to be "a gentle morality in harmony with nature that will regenerate the old world." He became a militant.

The strike in Carmaux had just failed, killed by politicians, leaving the workers weakened and starving. In the general depression Émile Henry decided to make heard a voice more fearful and virile than that of speechmakers: dynamite. It told the defeated who the real revolutionaries were; it told the victors that outside the speechifiers and the passive crowd, there were men who knew how to act.

Then came the Vaillant Affair (who was guillotined for having thrown a bomb in the Chamber of Deputies). The repression was frightful; in just a few days, mass arrests, searches, confiscation of publications, and expulsions decimated the ranks of the propagandists. The rebels were hunted down. Henry responded with an act: the bomb in the Café Terminus.

He was arrested.

At the hearings his calm and tranquility were disconcerting. The newspapers said this was either cynicism or an act. Not at all! It was the satisfied awareness of someone certain of having lived a useful and beautiful life. An actor? It's a strange actor who throws his head to the spectators.

For his judges, he had subtle raillery, astounding responses. When the president of the tribunal evoked Henry's bloodstained hands, Henry pointed at his red robe. When the same man reproached him for having abandoned a military career begun at the École Polytechnique, he had this marvelous response: "A beautiful career to be sure. One day they would have ordered me to fire on the unfortunate like Commandant Chapu at Fourmies. Thanks, but I'd rather be here."

Up to the guillotine, he remained as good, as brave. And can anyone say that such an end wasn't worth more than the long labor of the submissive and pointless death in a hospice or on a park bench? To be sure, there are other struggles that are less bloody and perhaps more useful; to be sure, speech that inspires enthusiasm, the written word, the invincible propagator of ideas, and above all a life spreading examples of love and fraternity are means of combat that are more beautiful. But to end by delivering an axe blow to the crumbling edifice, to end with the consciousness of having contributed even a bit to the great labor of emancipation, was a hundred times better that the idiotic death of a worker filling the bosses' safes.

On the gallows, his dry throat launched at the radiant May sun a cry of hope and bravery that the sound of the blade couldn't stifle: "Courage, comrades! Vive l'Anarchie!"

It was a death whose memory will live on. A death that free men will later remember with gratitude. For alongside the people of our century, the arrivistes, crushers, deceivers of all kinds, the immense mass of imbecilic followers and serfs, this young man marching toward death when everything in him wanted to live, this young man dying for the ideal is truly a luminous figure.

His blood was a beautiful seed from which new fighters will be born. And someday soon, when the wind will spread fire and construct barricades, the bourgeois who thought they'd crushed the new idea with bullets and guillotines will see the fatal harvest bloom.

Yes, anarchy is an ideal of peace and happiness. Yes, we love men with an infinite love, and every drop of their blood causes us pain. And it's because we love them, because we want to see them free, good, and happy, that we are merciless toward everything that blocks the road of humanity on its march toward the light!

From *Le Communiste* 13, May 23, 1908. Victor Serge was a seventeen-year-old anarchist militant in Belgium when he wrote this article for *Le Communiste*, to which he was a regular contributor.

■ SANTO CASERIO

The Trial of Santo Caserio

Recalling the childhood of Caserio, the president said to him, "You attended school but you never received any prizes." Caserio answered, "I regret not having had more education. I would have been stronger."

Q: And what would you have done with that strength?
A: I would have used it for the ideal.

Questioned about his relations with the lawyer Gori, he answered: "I didn't frequent Gori's conferences in 1891, but I read pamphlets and I paid closer attention to what was in them than to those he signed. In any case, I will lay out my doctrines."[1]

The president then asked him about his relations with the Italian anarchists, but Caserio remained silent on this point. "I am a baker," he said, "not a policeman . . ."

---

1 Pietro Gori (1865–1911) was a key figure of Italian anarchism. Twice exiled from Italy for his activities, he founded the anarchist review *Il Pensiero*.

Q: Recount your crime, Caserio.

A: At the moment when the last cavalrymen of the escort passed in front of me, I opened my jacket. The dagger was in the inside right-hand pocket, against my chest, with the handle up. I grabbed it with my left hand and with one movement shoved the two young people standing in front of me, took the handle with my right hand, and with my left pushed off the sheath, which fell to the ground. I quickly, but without leaping, headed straight for the president, following an oblique line in the direction opposite that of the carriage's movement. I put my left hand on the edge of the carriage and, with a slightly downward blow, my palm backward and my fingers pointed down, I plunged my dagger into the president's breast up to the hilt. (*And Caserio, with an unspeakable cynicism, demonstrated the way he used the dagger against the president.*) My hand touched his jacket. I left the dagger in the president's chest and a piece of newspaper remained on the handle. In delivering the blow I shouted—loudly or not, I don't know—"Vive la Révolution!" When I struck him M. Carnot looked me in the face. I then retreated, shouting "Vive la Révolution."

Q: You said that the president's look produced a strong sensation in you.

A: I felt no emotion.

Q: You wanted to strike him in the heart but your blow was delivered lower than you'd thought. Once the blow was delivered you fled. Seeing that you weren't immediately arrested and that no one seemed to have understood what you'd done, you started running, shouting "Vive l'Anarchie." You were going to disappear in the crowd. They refused to let you pass. Someone behind you shouted, "Arrest him!" Twenty policemen grabbed you and locked you up in a secure place. (*M. Breuillac then told of M. Carnot's final moments. The best doctors of our city did all they could to save so precious a life.*) The result of your dagger blow, Caserio, was M. Carnot's death. You know this?

A: (*In a weak voice*) Yes, I know.

Q: And it's because you are an anarchist that you killed M. Carnot. You hate all heads of state?

A: Yes, sir.

Q: You premeditated your crime. You admit this.

A: I'll answer in my declaration.

Ending his questioning the president of the tribunal said to Caserio, "Outside your political crime you killed a mother and father." Caserio then expounded at length in Italian. "No one had pity for the wives and children of the anarchists guillotined in France, hung in America, shot by firing squads in Spain." The interpreter was hardly able to translate the accused's words, which he mangled, giving rise to protests from the journalists.

From *L'Assassinat du President Carnot* by A. Lacassagne (Lyon: A. Storck/Paris: G. Masson, 1894).

Caserio's Defense Speech

Gentlemen of the jury, I'm not going to defend myself but rather explain my action.

While still young I learned that today's society is poorly organized, so poorly that every day many unfortunates commit suicide, leaving wives and children in the most terrible distress. Workers in their thousands look for work and can't find any. Poor families beg for their food and shiver from the cold. They suffer the worst poverty. The youngest ask their poor mothers for food and the latter can't give them any because they don't have anything. The few things that were in the house were already sold or traded. All they can do is ask for alms; they're often arrested for vagabondage.

I left my native land because I was often brought to tears upon seeing little girls of eight or ten forced to work fifteen hours a day for a miserable wage of twenty centimes. Young women of eighteen or twenty also work twenty hours a day for a laughable salary. And this doesn't only happen to my compatriots, but to all workers who sweat all day long for a morsel of bread while their labor brings in money in abundance. The workers are forced to live under the most wretched conditions and their food consists of a bit of bread, a few spoonfuls of rice, and water. And so when they reach the age of thirty or forty they're dying of fatigue and die in hospitals. What's more, as a consequence of their poor diets and overwork these sad creature are devoured in their hundreds by pellagra, an illness that, in my country, attacks, as the doctors say, those who are malnourished and who lead a hard and deprived existence.

I saw that there are some people who are hungry and some children who suffer while food and clothing are abundant in the cities. I saw several great industries full of clothing and wool products and I also saw warehouses full of wheat and corn that would be suitable for those who needed them. And from another point of view, I saw thousands of people who don't work, who produce nothing, and who live thanks to the labor of others; who every day spend thousands of francs to amuse themselves; who corrupt the daughters of workers; who own lodgings with forty or fifty rooms, twenty or thirty horses, and several servants: in a word, all the pleasures of life.

I believe in God, but when I see such inequality among men I recognize that it isn't God who created man but man who created God. And I discovered that those who want their property respected have an interest in preaching paradise and hell and keeping the people in a state of ignorance.

A short time ago, Vaillant threw a bomb in the Chamber of Deputies in protest against the current system of society. He killed no one and only wounded a few people. But bourgeois justice condemned him to death. And not satisfied with the condemnation of the guilty man, it pursued the anarchists and arrested not only those who knew Vaillant but even those who attended an anarchist lecture.

The government didn't think of their wives and children. It didn't consider that a man held in a cell isn't the only one to suffer, that his little ones ask for bread. Bourgeois justice didn't trouble itself with these innocents, who don't even know what society is. It's not their fault if their fathers are in prison; all they want to do is eat.

The government went so far as to search people's private homes, to open personal letters, to prohibit lectures and meetings and practiced the most infamous oppression against us. Even today hundreds of anarchists are arrested for having written an article in a newspaper or for having expressed an opinion in public.

Well then, if the government employs guns, chains, and prisons against us, must we anarchists, who defend our lives, remain locked in our houses? No. On the contrary, we answer governments with dynamite, bombs, the stylus, and the dagger. In a word, we must do all we can to destroy the bourgeoisie and government. Gentlemen of the jury, you who are the representatives of bourgeois society, if you want my head, take it. But don't think that in doing so you are stopping the anarchist movement.

Beware: man reaps what he sows.

From *L'Assassinat du President Carnot* by A. Lacassagne.

◼ CODA: SIMON RADOWITZKY

Argentina: Simon Radowitzky, Martyr of Anarchism

Though we've focused here on the propagandists of the deed in France, wherever there were anarchists, there were men willing to kill in order to bring down those in authority and to avenge victims of repression. The most celebrated among them were Leon Czolgosz, who killed President McKinley in 1901, and the Italian anarchist Gaetano Bresci, who assassinated King Umberto I in 1900. Argentina (the country with the most militant working-class movement in South America) had a well-entrenched anarchist movement, strongly influenced by immigrants from Italy, Spain, and Russia, who brought with them their utter devotion to the cause of ridding the world of exploiters. There, Simon Radowitzky, a young Ukrainian Jewish immigrant, became perhaps the purest symbol of this school of anarchist fighters, perhaps of all of anarchy. And while almost all the anarchist avengers went to their deaths on the scaffold, Radowitzky escaped execution, and his martyrdom—and heroism—went on for decades.

The events concerning him began on May Day 1909 in Buenos Aires, where two separate rallies occurred, one organized by the Socialists, the other by the anarchists.

Ramon Falcón, the city's police chief, was on the scene at the latter, more militant gathering. The demonstrators recognized him and shouted insults at him, along with cries of "War on the Bourgeoisie." The atmosphere became heated, until finally someone fired. It's uncertain whether the police first fired on the workers or the workers on the police, but the result was a police fusillade and a massacre, with 11 anarchists killed and 105 wounded.

Despite the outrage that followed the attack and the strikes called by workers' groups of all stripes to protest the killings and demand action against the police chief, Falcón suffered no consequences. Accordingly, a group of anarchists decided to act where the government and courts had failed to. On November 14, 1909, Falcón was assassinated in his car while on his way to work from the funeral of a prison employee. The assassin, captured on the spot, told his captors that he had no fear, since "I have a bomb for each of you."

The assassin was Simon Radowitzky, who had immigrated to Argentina in 1908 after having participated in his native Kiev in the revolutionary events of 1905. Under questioning, Radowitzky refused to name any accomplices, and when placed on trial took full credit for his act, explaining in a declaration that would be published under the title "Why I Killed":

> I killed because on May 1, 1909, Colonel Falcón, at the head of the American Cossacks, led the massacre of the workers. My indignation reached its paroxysm when I suffered the shame of realizing that the people's representatives in the Chambers applauded the attitude of the cited police chief.

I am the son of the working people, brother of those who fell in the struggle with the bourgeoisie, and like everyone my soul suffered for the agony of those who died that evening solely for believing in the advent of a freer and better future for humanity.

The death penalty was sought and expected, but investigation revealed that Radowitzky, who, upon his capture, was thought to be in his twenties, was in reality eighteen, and so not eligible for the death penalty. He was instead sentenced to life in the Argentine Siberia, Ushuaia, in Tierra del Fuego. The cold, the wind, the wretched food and conditions were all made worse by the fact that every November 14, the anniversary of his attentat, he was made to spend three weeks in isolation. Beatings weren't enough: the prison directors were accused of encouraging other prisoners to rape Radowitzky.

His comrades hadn't forgotten him, and a campaign in his favor was maintained throughout his imprisonment. Ushuaia was not only Siberia, it was the Argentine Devil's Island, a place from which escape was thought to be impossible—until a group of Radowitzky's comrades assisted his escape on a boat on the Beagle Canal. Radowitzky was soon captured and returned to prison, but his escape added to his myth.

Throughout his time in prison, Radowitzky fought not only against the conditions under which he was forced to live, but also those to which his fellow prisoners were subjected. His description of life in Ushuaia was published in a pamphlet called *La Voz de Mi Conciencia* (The Voice of My Conscience), in which he described the cruelty and barbarity of the prison and its keepers.

Compañeros: Bear in mind that what I am telling you in this letter is only a part of what I heard and saw in the twelve years that I was imprisoned in Pavilion no. 5. There were the beatings in the dungeons below my cell and hearing the cries caused by blows and hunger! To tell you the truth, when I was healthy, the food, the half rations weren't enough for me. There were nights when I couldn't sleep for hunger. And to think that below my cell there were others who didn't have even a drop of water or a mattress . . . stretched out on the ground on winter nights . . . the screams, the cries! It was truly enough to drive you mad, and there was my torment when they took out Bugatto and put a madman in the cell, prisoner no. 406, who, as a result of his seclusion, imprisonment, and beatings, lost his reason and spent day and night repeating this refrain: "The truth is my truths are our truths and the truths I speak are true truths." Since it was impossible for me to go on like this, since I couldn't sleep because of the "truths" he sang in a loud voice, I asked that my cell be changed. I was answered: "That's how he amuses himself and he doesn't get bored, but if you'd like, we can tell the administration." Do you know what they did? They saw to it that things got worse, that I didn't eat and slept little, and every night at midnight and 4:00 a.m. they opened my cell door and woke me up, saying, "How are you?" I asked that at least during the night they leave me in peace and they answered that the order from above was to look in on me twice a night from "fear" that I'd hang myself. . . . And for more than a year, there are thirty in my cell with its madman who chants to me "the truth is my truths, etc., etc."

But he wasn't the only madman. Before there was another one, but an odd one.

He dreamed and raved, woke up calling for help, and called out to me in his poor Spanish mixed with Italian, "Simon, untie the nerves that they have taken me away and moored my *cuore*," he cried, he shouted. The guards, the idiots, came during the night to have fun with him. There was another who raved that they'd killed his wife and children. A police official in Cordoba had dishonored this man's daughter and drove her into a brothel. Upon learning of this, he killed the official and was sentenced to twenty-five years in prison. Since coming here, he lost his mind. At first, as was customary, they said he was feigning madness, but it's now been three years that he's demented and they haven't done a thing for him! It's truly incomprehensible that he hasn't died from the ill-treatment he's suffered. He'll never recover his reason. I don't know his name; his number is 273.

From November 30, 1918, until January 7, 1921, I was within four walls without seeing the light of day and on half rations. This was one of the four spells of solitary confinement I suffered. The first was from March 1912 until October 1913; the second from February 1914 until December; and the third from October 1915 until May 25, 1916. During each confinement I was at first held to twenty or thirty days of bread and water. Later, when I worked, I received many blows to the head. . . .

On January 3, at mealtime, the inspector from the Ministry of Justice Dr. Victor Barón Peña introduced himself to me in my cell. He asked me my name. I told him. Even though he already knew who I was he asked it in order to be sure.

"Are you an inspector from Justice?"

"Yes."

I wanted to speak but he told me to keep on eating and that he'd call on me the following day. Which he did.

The next evening I was called to the director's office and I must confess that I barely had the strength to walk there and remain upright. The inspector gave me a chair, where I sat in order to make my declaration. I spoke. I spoke a lot. I recounted all I'd seen and suffered since the day I'd arrived in the prison. All the solitary confinements, the dungeons, and the persecutions to which the prisoners are victim. He listened to me closely and told me that everything would change, that he'd come with a humanitarian mission and to see that justice was done. I told him that when people came and intervened the prisoners were treated well, and the next day, after having seen off the visitors for their return to the capital, the prison returned to its former methods.

He assured me that this time that wouldn't be the case and that he'd ensure that the orders he'd give that the prisoners would be treated humanely would be met. After me, all the prisoners paraded before him. Some of them collapsed on the way to the office, so the inspector went to the cells and there the man had to make an effort to hold back his tears when hearing a prisoner tell him that, for having asked the chief of service, Gonzalez, that he be treated because he was ill, and for having said this from his window, he was held for thirty-seven days on bread and water (as I write this he is dying; yesterday myself and another comrade took him to the sick bay); and the unheard of suffering of others who went mad from hunger and beatings; others who spent more than two years without a shirt; and others (a madman who they insulted) who, for having spoken through the window spent thirty days on bread and water; and whenever he fancied it, Sanpedro filled the dungeons.[1] The inspector is truly worthy of admiration: compañeros, he did honor to justice. Until one in the morning, he went from building to building, from cell to cell. He suspended Palacios and Rocha,[2] fired six guards, and on January 7 lifted solitary confinement on all those in Pavilion no. 5. Unfortunately for me and other prisoners, he opened the gates a little late, but at the very least I will have the satisfaction upon dying of having seen a human being and the light of day.

And not only did the inspector—who was a man, an honorable man—do this. The day he spoke to me, when he took me from the cell, I told him that if he wanted proof of the beatings administered in the dungeons in the building in which I was held he could see the sticks and a truncheon filled with sand. I told him where they were kept and he went there, found them, and found something else.

The members of the administration, that is Palacios and Rocha, told him that the garrotes belonged to the prisoners (when he found the garrotes he was presented to the Chief of the Guards José Muzzo, and

---

1 Another chief guard at Ushuaia.
2 Prison administrators.

when the inspector asked him why the garrotes were there he wasn't able to answer, standing there dumbfounded) and that we had firearms, knives, daggers, etc.

The following day, the inspector ordered all the personnel to present themselves at 3:00 a.m. They thought this was a new procedure or some maneuver. At three the inspector appeared and gave the order to search the cells. The search, carried out in the presence of the inspector, lasted from three until nine, and all that was found were cigarette lighters. The inspector laughed and asked if cigarette lighters were considered firearms here and if the knives weren't anything but a few pieces of tin that the prisoners used for cutting their meat. They then understood that the inspector hadn't come to hear the marching band and to participate in banquets, so the guards and a few prisoners began to foment discord in the pavilions, advising the prisoners not to go to work. But all the convicts realized what was going on and denounced to the inspector the guards who were causing disorder and were rousing the prisoners to revolt. All of their efforts were useless: the prisoners were united and behaved correctly when making their declarations.

A few days later a commission composed of four deputies arrived on the cruiser "San Martín." They first went to Pavilion no. 5. Upon their arrival at my cell they asked me why there was so much persecution in the prison. I spoke for more than two hours, describing everything: how we were treated there, the punishments, the solitary confinement, etc. I wasn't able to speak longer, having a sore throat, which cut off my voice. They went to the other cells and were horrified at seeing the other internees. They said: "The notoriety of this prison is truly justified." When they went to the sick bay, where almost all of the patients were victims from Pavilion no. 5, they fled, not being able to bear the sight of the dying or the tuberculars, spitting up blood.

Comrade workers: in the name of all those they met in the prison, my comrades in misfortune, we salute you and thank you for your initiatives against the crimes in this somber prison.

Simon Radowitzky
Ushuaia Prison, January 1921

PS: The prison now functions normally but . . . yesterday a new regulation was implemented from which it appears that we will return to how things were before. We'll see.

The years passed, and the campaign to free him never let up, the walls of Buenos Aires covered with the graffiti *"Libertad a Radowitzky!"* So strong was the adulation of his comrades that an anarchist newspaper headlined an article about him, "The Christ of the Twentieth Century."

Visited in prison by a journalist, the latter wrote of him: "He knows that as an anarchist he continues to enjoy popularity and that his comrades have placed on him the crown of a martyr, but he says that he's bothered by such demonstrations and that he didn't kill Falcón to become famous, but rather impelled by his beliefs."

Finally, in May 1930, President Yrigoyen pardoned Radowitzky (in order to prevent his liberation causing anger among the police and army his name was included among 110 others) and he was deported by ship to Uruguay.

There, he continued his anarchist activities that again led him to prison, this time in the prison on the Isla de Flores. As in Argentina, a campaign in his favor was initiated in which all elements of the Left joined. Perhaps nothing better expresses the purity of Radowitzky's life and ideals than the open letter he sent to the Uruguayan Communist Party and its affiliated unions, refusing their support:

> To the Communist Party and the National Confederation of Labor:
>
> I have learned of your propaganda and posters, in which my name figures demanding my freedom.
>
> As an anarchist I say to you: I declare that I don't wish to be the propaganda instrument of any political party, including the Communist Party, whose support of the policies of the Russian government is absolute.
>
> In the name of the anarchists prisoner in prisons and Soviet Siberia; in the name of the destroyed anarchist groups whose propaganda is prohibited in Russia; in the name of the comrades executed at Kronstadt; in the name of our comrade Petrini who was handed over to Italian fascism by the Soviet government; in the name of the Argentine Regional Workers' Federation and the Uruguayan Regional Workers' Federation; in the name of our comrades killed in prison by the Bolshevik government; and in protest against the calumnies and defamation against our comrades Kropotkin, Malatesta, Rocker, Fabbri, Makhno, etc., etc., I declare that as an anarchist I reject all of your support, which represents an unworthy exploitation on the part of the Bolshevik leaders of the party and

the CGT of the generous sentiment of solidarity shown
me by the working class.

Simon Radowitzky, Montevideo

Finally released in 1936, Radowitzky, now forty-six,
went to Spain to join the anarchists in fighting Franco's
rebellion, working in the foreign propaganda section of the
anarchist CNT in Barcelona. Writing to comrades in 1938
as bombs were falling he said that, "I am calm and more
optimistic than ever of our victory."

Forced to flee in 1939, responsible for transport-
ing the CNT's archives, he joined his comrades in their
retreat across Spain and into France, where he wrote to an
Uruguayan comrade, "[after] one terrible night there were
twenty dead of hunger and cold," and having nothing to
eat "we were able to rob some rice and chickpeas guarded
by the gendarmes." Thoroughly Argentine, he also wrote,
"we also had some mate because Reynolda [a comrade] had
some yerba."

After a brief stay in France, he joined the exodus of
Republican supporters to Mexico. From there, he wrote to
the same Uruguayan comrade that "it is extremely probable that I'm going to work in a factory as a . . . peon." He
spent his last years in Mexico working in a toy factory,
writing for and distributing anarchist journals. He changed
his name to José Gomez and died of a heart attack in 1956.
His Mexican comrades had to take up a collection to pay
for his funeral.

■ ABOUT MITCHELL ABIDOR

Mitchell Abidor is the principal French translator for the Marxists Internet Archive and has published several collections of his translations, including *Anarchists Never Surrender: Essays, Polemics, and Correspondence on Anarchism* by Victor Serge. He is currently working on translations of further unpublished works by Victor Serge and Daniel Guérin.

ABOUT PM PRESS

PM Press was founded at the end of 2007 by a small collection of folks with decades of publishing, media, and organizing experience. PM Press co-conspirators have published and distributed hundreds of books, pamphlets, CDs, and DVDs. Members of PM have founded enduring book fairs, spearheaded victorious tenant organizing campaigns, and worked closely with bookstores, academic conferences, and even rock bands to deliver political and challenging ideas to all walks of life. We're old enough to know what we're doing and young enough to know what's at stake.

We seek to create radical and stimulating fiction and non-fiction books, pamphlets, T-shirts, visual and audio materials to entertain, educate, and inspire you. We aim to distribute these through every available channel with every available technology—whether that means you are seeing anarchist classics at our bookfair stalls; reading our latest vegan cookbook at the café; downloading geeky fiction e-books; or digging new music and timely videos from our website.

PM Press is always on the lookout for talented and skilled volunteers, artists, activists, and writers to work with. If you have a great idea for a project or can contribute in some way, please get in touch.

PM Press
PO Box 23912
Oakland, CA 94623
www.pmpress.org

FRIENDS OF PM PRESS

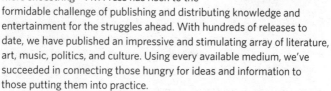

These are indisputably momentous times—the financial system is melting down globally and the Empire is stumbling. Now more than ever there is a vital need for radical ideas.

In the years since its founding—and on a mere shoestring—PM Press has risen to the formidable challenge of publishing and distributing knowledge and entertainment for the struggles ahead. With hundreds of releases to date, we have published an impressive and stimulating array of literature, art, music, politics, and culture. Using every available medium, we've succeeded in connecting those hungry for ideas and information to those putting them into practice.

Friends of PM allows you to directly help impact, amplify, and revitalize the discourse and actions of radical writers, filmmakers, and artists. It provides us with a stable foundation from which we can build upon our early successes and provides a much-needed subsidy for the materials that can't necessarily pay their own way. You can help make that happen—and receive every new title automatically delivered to your door once a month—by joining as a Friend of PM Press. And, we'll throw in a free T-shirt when you sign up.

Here are your options (all include a 50% discount on all webstore purchases):
- **$30 a month** Get all books and pamphlets
- **$40 a month** Get all PM Press releases (including CDs and DVDs)
- **$100 a month** Everything plus PM merchandise and free downloads

For those who can't afford $30 or more a month, we're introducing **Sustainer Rates** at $15, $10 and $5. Sustainers get a free PM Press T-shirt and a 50% discount on all purchases from our website.

Your Visa or Mastercard will be billed once a month, until you tell us to stop. Or until our efforts succeed in bringing the revolution around. Or the financial meltdown of Capital makes plastic redundant. Whichever comes first.

Anarchists Never Surrender: Essays, Polemics, and Correspondence on Anarchism, 1908–1938

Victor Serge • Editor: Mitchell Abidor • Foreword: Richard Greeman

ISBN: 978-1-62963-031-1
$20.00 • 256 Pages

Anarchists Never Surrender provides a complete picture of Victor Serge's relationship to anarchism. The volume contains writings going back to his teenage years in Brussels, where he became influenced by the doctrine of individualist anarchism. At the heart of the anthology are key articles written soon after his arrival in Paris in 1909, when he became editor of the newspaper *l'anarchie*. In these articles Serge develops and debates his own radical thoughts, arguing the futility of mass action and embracing "illegalism." Serge's involvement with the notorious French group of anarchist armed robbers, the Bonnot Gang, landed him in prison for the first time in 1912. *Anarchists Never Surrender* includes both his prison correspondence with his anarchist comrade Émile Armand and articles written immediately after his release.

The book also includes several articles and letters written by Serge after he had left anarchism behind and joined the Russian Bolsheviks in 1919. Here Serge analyzed anarchism and the ways in which he hoped anarchism would leaven the harshness and dictatorial tendencies of Bolshevism. Included here are writings on anarchist theory and history, Bakunin, the Spanish revolution, and the Kronstadt uprising.

Anarchists Never Surrender anthologizes Victor Serge's previously unavailable texts on anarchism and fleshes out the portrait of this brilliant writer and thinker, a man I.F. Stone called one of the "moral figures of our time."

"One of the most compelling of twentieth-century ethical and literary heroes."
—Susan Sontag

Outrage:
An Anarchist Memoir of the
Penal Colony

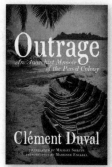

Clément Duval
Translator: Michael Shreve
Introduction: Marianne Enckell

ISBN: 978-1-60486-500-4
$20.00 • 224 Pages

"Theft exists only through the exploitation of man by man...when Society refuses you the right to exist, you must take it...the policeman arrested me in the name of the Law, I struck him in the name of Liberty."

In 1887, Clément Duval joined the tens of thousands of convicts sent to the "dry guillotine" of the French penal colonies. Few survived and fewer were able to tell the stories of their life in that hell. Duval spent fourteen years doing hard labor—espousing the values of anarchism and demonstrating the ideals by being a living example the entire time—before making his daring escape and arriving in New York City, welcomed by the Italian and French anarchists there.

This is much more than an historical document about the anarchist movement and the penal colony. It is a remarkable story of survival by one man's self-determination, energy, courage, loyalty, and hope. It was thanks to being true and faithful to his ideals that Duval survived life in this hell. Unlike the well-known prisoner Papillon, who arrived and dramatically escaped soon after Duval, he encouraged his fellow prisoners to practice mutual aid, through their deeds and not just their words. It is a call to action for mindful, conscious people to fight for their rights to the very end, to never give up or give in.

More than just a story of a life or a testament of ideals, here is a monument to the human spirit and a war cry for freedom and justice.

Anarchy, Geography, Modernity: Selected Writings of Elisée Reclus

Elisée Reclus

Editors: John P. Clark and
Camille Martin

ISBN: 978-1-60486-429-8
$22.95 • 304 Pages

Anarchy, Geography, Modernity is the first
comprehensive introduction to the thought of Elisée Reclus, the great
anarchist geographer and political theorist. It shows him to be an
extraordinary figure for his age. Not only an anarchist but also a radical
feminist, anti-racist, ecologist, animal rights advocate, cultural radical,
nudist, and vegetarian. Not only a major social thinker but also a
dedicated revolutionary.

The work analyzes Reclus' greatest achievement, a sweeping historical
and theoretical synthesis recounting the story of the earth and
humanity as an epochal struggle between freedom and domination. It
presents his groundbreaking critique of all forms of domination: not
only capitalism, the state, and authoritarian religion, but also patriarchy,
racism, technological domination, and the domination of nature. His
crucial insights on the interrelation between personal and small-
group transformation, broader cultural change, and large-scale social
organization are explored. Reclus' ideas are presented both through
detailed exposition and analysis, and in extensive translations of key
texts, most appearing in English for the first time.

*"Maintaining an appropriately scholarly style, marked by deep background
knowledge, nuanced argument, and careful qualifications, Clark and
Martin nevertheless reveal a passionate love for their subject and adopt a
stance of political engagement that they hope does justice to Reclus' own
commitments."*
—*Historical Geography*

Voices of the Paris Commune

Editor: Mitchell Abidor

ISBN: 978-1-62963-100-4
$14.95 • 128 Pages

The Paris Commune of 1871, the first instance of a working-class seizure of power, has been subject to countless interpretations; reviled by its enemies as a murderous bacchanalia of the unwashed while praised by supporters as an exemplar of proletarian anarchism in action. As both a successful model to be imitated and as a devastating failure to be avoided. All of the interpretations are tendentious. Historians view the working class's three-month rule through their own prism, distant in time and space. *Voices of the Paris Commune* takes a different tack. In this book only those who were present in the spring of 1871, who lived through and participated in the Commune, are heard.

The Paris Commune had a vibrant press, and it is represented here by its most important newspaper, *Le Cri du Peuple*, edited by Jules Vallès, member of the First International. Like any legitimate government, the Paris Commune held parliamentary sessions and issued daily printed reports of the heated, contentious deliberations that belie any accusation of dictatorship. Included in this collection is the transcript of the debate in the Commune, just days before its final defeat, on the establishing of a Committee of Public Safety and on the fate of the hostages held by the Commune, hostages who would ultimately be killed.

Finally, *Voices of the Paris Commune* contains a selection from the inquiry carried out twenty years after the event by the intellectual review La Revue Blanche, asking participants to judge the successes and failures of the Paris Commune. This section provides a fascinating range of opinions of this epochal event.

"The Paris Commune of 1871 has been the subject of much ideological debate, often far removed from the experiences of the participants themselves. If you really want to dig deep into what happened during those fateful weeks, reading these eyewitness accounts is mandatory."
—Gabriel Kuhn, editor of *All Power to the Councils! A Documentary History of the German Revolution of 1918–1919*